Best of Breed

THE SIBERIAN HUSKY

Your Essential Guide
From Puppy To
Senior Dog

Edited By
**Nicky Hutchison
& Helen Wood**

ACKNOWLEDGEMENTS

The publishers would like to thank the Siberian Husky Club of America (http://www.shca.org/) and Forstal Siberian Huskies (http://www.huskyrides.co.uk/) for many of the pictures in *Chapter Two: The First Siberian Huskies*. Special thanks are also due to Helen Wood (www.siberprint.co.uk), Chris McRae and Lesley Howarth who provided many of the photographs throughout this book. The publishers would also like to thank Rachael Prince, Cushla Lamen, Anita Davidson, Chris Heald and Catherine Lewis for additional photography.

All photography taken for the purpose of this book required dogs to be on a lead for safety reasons, unless being taken in an enclosed area. However, some photographs have been digitally altered and had leads removed for artistic reasons. Please keep your Siberian Husky on a lead at all times.

Cover photo: © Tracy Morgan Animal Photography (www.animalphotographer.co.uk)
Dog featured is Penkhala's Arion ('Ron') owned by Yricka Gardner.

The British Breed Standard reproduced in Chapter 7 is the copyright of the Kennel Club and published with the club's kind permission. Extracts from the American Breed Standard are reproduced by kind permission of the American Kennel Club.

THE QUESTION OF GENDER
The 'he' pronoun is used throughout this book instead of the rather impersonal 'it', but no gender bias is intended.

First published in 2012 by the Pet Book Publishing Company Limited
St Martin's Farm, Chapel Lane, Zeals, Wiltshire BA12 6NZ

This edition first published in 2015

© 2015 Pet Book Publishing Company Limited.
Printed and bound in South Korea.

ISBN
978-1-910488-06-5
1-910488-06-2

CONTENTS

GETTING TO KNOW SIBERIAN HUSKIES

S o you think you want a Siberian Husky? Or you have just bought a Siberian Husky and want to know what you have let yourself in for…

Obviously you already know that they are the smartest, most marvellous, best-looking dog ever, but what makes them so special? What are their drawbacks? How do you adapt to life with such an unusual dog? No matter what your dog trainer/neighbour/ parents tell you, huskies are not the same as 'normal' dogs, however much you wish they were. But, in fact, most owners agree that it is all the hard work you have to put into them that makes them so worthwhile.

THE DIFFERENCES

So what are the main differences between the Siberian Husky and other breeds?

BRED TO PULL

This is a dog that has been bred to pull for thousands of years. If you want your arms to stay the same length, and your shoulders to remain in their sockets, buy a walking belt! With a little gentle persuasion, a Siberian Husky can be taught to walk reasonably nicely – but not to stop pulling. It is their job. It would be like buying a retriever and then expecting it not to retrieve! You could see this as a drawback, or you could just accept that it is great for keeping you fit!

A COAT THAT SHEDS

Twice a year, truly ridiculous amounts of fur will fall out of your dog. Until it first happens, you have no real concept of how much fur a Siberian Husky is actually made up of. It gets in your food, up your nose, on every item of your clothing, hanging in the very air you breathe. Coat shedding lasts for several weeks, and you could knit a whole new dog from the fur that is deposited in your home. Some people do knit with it. It is also great for birds to line their nests with. Your neighbours may be less keen on it blowing across their gardens like tumbleweed and attaching itself to their washing. Groom your dog inside, and buy a Dyson!

It has been said that people with dog allergies are less affected by huskies, but too many of them have ended up in rescue because their owner has proved to be allergic for me to be convinced by this.

FREE SPIRITS

Given the opportunity, Siberian Huskies will run (and hunt) until they are exhausted. If you let your husky off the lead, he will probably be several miles away by

This is a breed like no other, but if you find the Siberian suits you, you'll be hooked for life.

the time this happens. This is very bad. There will probably be several roads in the way (the breed has a particular lack of road sense), fields of sheep, possibly an annoyed farmer with a shotgun, and almost certainly an ex-cat or two.

If you are one of those people who find it inconvenient to take their dogs for proper walks, or thinks it is cruel to keep them on leads, please buy another, more trainable breed.

DESTRUCTIVE URGE
Siberian Huskies will entertain themselves if left to their own devices. For some reason, it is always the things that you most want to keep that they most want to destroy. On the plus side, it will teach you – and your kids – to keep the house tidy…

It cannot be stressed enough that you have to adapt to the breed's character traits, not the other way round. If you think your dog will be different, you are

likely to be sadly disappointed and your dog may well end up in rescue, or worse. If, however, you have read and accepted all this, and still want a Siberian Husky, be prepared for your life to change – hopefully for the better!

PHYSICAL CHARACTERISTICS
Unlike so many other breeds today, the Siberian Husky is relatively unchanged from the early years in which the breed was first standardised. This is more

than likely because, again, unlike a lot of other breeds, many huskies still perform the original function that the breed was designed for, i.e, to pull. The requirements of the Breed Standard, the written blueprint for the breed, are based on what is needed for a good, working dog, which influences every aspect of the breed's physical and mental make-up.

Movement should be smooth and effortless; a Siberian Husky should be light on his feet, balanced and graceful, never cobby or thickset. He should be double-coated, with a soft, dense undercoat, and an outer coat of straight, smooth guard hairs, which should not be long or shaggy, nor stand off straight from the body. The Siberian is one of the few breeds for which absolutely any colour, or combination of colours and markings is acceptable.

The Siberian male should be 53 to 60 cm (21-23.5 in) tall at the withers, or top of the shoulders, and weigh 20 to 27 kg (45-60 lb). Bitches should be 51 to 56 cm (20-22 in), and weigh 16 to 23 kg (35-50 lb). Many Siberians go through an awkward teenage stage, where their legs and ears appear to belong to a different dog, and it can be very hard to keep weight on them at this stage. Feeding extra food frequently results in a case of the 'runs'. But by the time the dog matures, usually at about two years old, he should be well muscled without looking bulky, and his ribs should have a decent covering.

The exhibitor with no interest in running their dogs may not see any need to take working ability into account when breeding purely for the show ring. In the same way, some working owners who do not show their dogs think the standard has no relevance for them, and breed exclusively for working ability. However, this is the start of the slippery slope that many former working breeds have found themselves on. At best, the breed splits into two types, which barely look like the same dog – the working strains retaining the athletic abilities that the show strains gradually lose. At worst, where the original purpose of the breed is lost altogether, the dogs can end up physically unable to do the job they were designed for. You would be waiting a long time for today's show Basset Hound to catch a hare, for example, or for a modern St Bernard to dig you out of an avalanche!

TEMPERAMENT

It is specified in the Breed Standard that the Siberian Husky should be friendly and outgoing, neither suspicious with strangers, nor aggressive with other dogs. Like so many other of their qualities, this goes back to their original use. The Chuckchi people, who developed the breed, often took them into their homes with their children. In the harsh working environment, a lead dog

The Siberian Husky has remained relatively unchanged since the breed was first developed.

The delightful, outgoing, friendly personality of the Siberian Husky is one of the most important aspects of the breed, so it is important to select parents with good temperaments.

would have to be extremely tough, and very high levels of deference would be demanded from lower ranking pack members – aggression and fighting on the team would not be tolerated. Miles from home, the ability of his team to work together could mean the difference between life and death for a dog driver.

Unless you want to find yourself unable to overtake another team on the trail without a punch up, or banned from the show ring because your dog has taken chunks out of the judge, it is very important to buy from lines with good, happy, outgoing temperaments. It is also clearly the most important consideration in a pet dog.

TYPICAL BEHAVIOUR

The Siberian Husky is a very easy-to-please dog; all he basically wants is to have company, to run fast, to pull stuff and to hunt things. Once you take this on board, you will be on the way to understanding your dog.

It doesn't matter if you have won all the rosettes for recall in your puppy training class. Many huskies will lull you into a false sense of security by being great at it for a while. But at some point, usually around the teenage phase of puberty, they will suddenly acquire the confidence to branch out from their pack, ie, you, and run off.

When people tell you not to let your Siberian off the lead in areas that don't have great big fences round them, it's not because they don't want your dog to have any fun. It's also not because they're

Although Siberians can never be trusted off the lead, in case of equipment failure it is very important to regularly practise emergency recalls in properly fenced areas.

too lazy to train theirs (giving them enough on-lead exercise is the very opposite of lazy), didn't "bond" with them as puppies, or bought the wrong lines or pedigrees. It's because they've seen dozens of people, convinced they and their dogs were different, pay for these delusions with the lives of their dogs.

This is not to say that you should not bother to practise the recall in a safe, enclosed space – you absolutely must. Accidents happen, and an emergency recall is

a vital trick to have up your sleeve.

The Siberian Husky is not a one-man dog, and is likely to kiss a burglar and show him where your valuables are. Many people who keep packs that live outside add a guarding breed for protection.

Few Siberians bark after they have passed the puppy stage – even if someone is breaking into your house! Quite a lot of them howl, however, which is a trait mainly confined to the more primitive breeds. Single dogs may howl if there is a bitch in season,

or if they are bored or lonely – a sort of "where are you?" message, going back to the original function of wolves howling to call the pack together.

Howling is more common in households with several Siberians, sometimes for no other reason than pure enjoyment. Encouraging it as a party trick can backfire – it can be very hard to stop once they get going, and they will just interpret your yelling as a rather tuneless attempt to join in!

Also in the Siberian vocabulary is

'woo-ing', which is usually caused by excitement, or when they are trying to tell you something.

Some Siberians make a sound similar to a growl when they are happy, which can be confusing and disconcerting for a new owner. In this case it is really important that you learn to read the other signals your dog is giving, in order to know which sort of growl it is.

THE HUSKY BRAIN

The Siberian Husky was developed as a dog that could think for himself, which can give him a reputation for being stubborn. The questioning intellect of the breed was a vital tool to the tribes that bred them. If the musher wanted his dog to go over a frozen lake, for example, the dog had to have the inbuilt sense to know whether it was dangerous, and the strength of character to refuse a direct command if necessary.

The majority of huskies are too intelligent for their own good! This is not a dog that can be left alone all day, or crated for hours on end. A bored husky is a destructive and noisy husky. A dog which does not get enough attention can end up with behavioural and emotional problems, and because the breed is quite sensitive, these can turn into physical problems, too. It is so much easier to stop a problem developing in the first place than to try to fix it later.

As long as his intelligence and energy are channelled into something useful, your husky will be a happy dog.

MORE THAN ONE?

Be careful you know what you are getting into when you buy your first Siberian Husky – they really do seem to be addictive…

If you are with your dog for the majority of the day, your company may be sufficient, but most Siberians are happier with a canine pack as well. Their canine friend does not have to be another husky, although you should bear in mind that huskies as a breed play in a particularly rough manner. Therefore, if a Siberian is kept with a smaller dog, you will need to ensure that play does not become too boisterous for the smaller dog to cope with.

This is a breed that inspires loyalty so if you find that their unique character suits you, you will probably never look at another breed again. Once you have one, you tend to end up with two, then three. Then you will be buying a house with more land so your huskies can run around in safety, and maybe a van to go to rallies in. Before you know it, you will be dreaming of moving to Alaska and running down to the shops on the sled.

Soon your social life will be populated, almost entirely, by other husky people because they do not mind the almost magical transfer of dog hairs from one person to another. Everybody else will get: "I'm sorry, I can't, I've got a rally/dog show that weekend…"

However, collecting Siberian

"Woo-ing" is a noise made almost exclusively by excited sled dogs!

Siberians seem to be a particularly addictive breed. If you have the facilities, you will soon find numbers mounting.

Huskies should be done over time. For some reason, the people who rush out and buy a six-dog team after their first rally are also the ones dumping that six-dog team in rescue after the novelty wears off.

It is not a good idea to get two puppies at the same time. People seem to have the idea that the pups will occupy each other and be less trouble, when, in fact, the reverse tends to be true. The puppies will bond with each other instead of you, and will wind each other up to a frenzy of naughtiness!

You should also be confident that you can get through their teenage 'spawn of satan' phase, without being driven insane, before you start adding to your pack. It is always better to get the behaviour of your first dog sorted out before you get a second. Buying another dog to entertain a bored, destructive dog who howls all day will simply result in two bored, destructive dogs who howl all day, neighbours who hate you, and possibly a visit from the council…

It is absolutely lovely to see a puppy watching older dogs and learning habits and the house rules from them. It is not lovely if they are learning to howl in harmony and eat your furniture!

A mixed pack can be a recipe for stress and sleepless nights, unless you have masses of space to separate the males and females during seasons, or intend to neuter at least one gender. Siberian males in particular can be highly sexed, leading to much tweeting and whining, and even fights between kennel-mates who usually get along well.

LIVING WITH OTHER ANIMALS

The Siberian Husky has an exceptionally strong prey drive, making the vast majority of them a danger to small, furry animals, birds and livestock. If you are wondering what use a pronounced hunting instinct is in developing a sled dog, it is there because the teams were turned loose in the summer to catch their own food.

If a Siberian puppy is brought up with the resident cat, he may get along with that particular animal, while still seeing a strange animal of the same species as lunch. But even with their 'own' cat, a Sibe can never entirely be trusted, so do not leave them alone in the same room when you are not there. Some huskies are fine when the cat is just pottering around the house, but their prey drive will get the better of them if the cat takes off across the garden at a run. Siberians have been known to kill cats they have lived happily with for years, for no obvious reason.

It is never a good idea to replace a cat when it dies, even if the dog has got on well with the one he grew up with.

SIBERIANS AND CHILDREN

It is frequently the smallest members of the household that set up the initial demand for a husky, usually after watching a film that portrays the breed in a wildly unrealistic light. The child's interest will probably move on after the dog passes its cute puppy stage, and you will be left with a pet that can live another 12-15 years, and takes a lot of work. It is therefore very important that all members of the family want the breed, and are realistic about the commitment that it entails.

Are Siberians good with children? Yes, mostly, but the more important question is are your kids going to understand the extra demands of owning a Siberian over a 'normal' dog? Are they old enough to be trusted not to open the door risking your dog dashing out into traffic? Can they

Most Siberians love children, although interactions should always be supervised.

keep their easily swallowed toys out of the dog's reach?

Children should be taught to be consistent and kind with the dog. If children mistreat animals, it is usually because their parents have neglected to teach them any better.

Even if your children are great with your Siberian Husky, they should never be left alone with him, and they certainly should not be allowed to walk him. A determined Siberian can pull over most adults, and it would be almost criminally unsafe to allow a child to walk him. If he dashed out into the road after a cat, would the child let go of the lead or not?

IN OR OUT?

Contrary to popular belief, Siberian Huskies do not need to live outside for the good of their coats. A Sibe will shed his coat twice a year wherever he lives.

You can shorten the process if you help the coat to come out with daily grooming. There are special dog combs and brushes made for double-coated breeds, which look a bit like a rake. You should use these, as equipment for shorthaired dogs may slice through the guard hairs while not efficiently removing the undercoat.

I have never seen the point of buying a pet dog then sticking it out in a kennel – a Siberian loves to be with you whatever you are doing. But if you decide to build your dog an outside run for periods when you may be out, make sure he has a warm, dry indoor area for sleeping, and plenty of shade for summer. Huskies are prone to sunbathe more than is good for them, and consequently overheat.

You will need 6 ft (1.82 m) fences to keep a Siberian in his run – and even higher for some dogs. Do not use trellis fencing, as your Siberian will think it's great to climb up. Be aware that some dogs will spend a lot of time trying to tunnel under fencing, so make sure that this is not possible. Your Sibe will appreciate a little platform to lie on and observe the world from a height – but make sure that nothing within the pen can be used as a springboard to escape over the top.

Introduce your Siberian Husky to his kennel gradually. Just as if you were introducing him to an indoor crate, feed him in there and let him wander in and out for a few days before you try shutting hm in for short periods of time. Make sure you provide a variety of toys to keep him occupied. However, if you intend to leave a lone Siberian in a kennel for hours on end, you will be lucky if you don't end up with a depressed dog, or annoyed neighbours.

An outside run should be securely fenced with access to shade and, preferably, a look-out platform.

FINDING OUT MORE

There are some great forums out there that can be an absolute lifesaver for the first-time Siberian owner. There are also some that seem to be peopled exclusively by idiots. Beware the five-minute expert, who knows everything about the breed within weeks of buying his first dog…

If you can find a good forum, it is a great way of making new Sibe friends in your local area, getting advice on events nearby, or the really important task of finding vets in your area with experience of Siberians. This is necessary because the breed is sensitive to some drugs, especially anaesthetics and sedatives. A Siberian has very little fat

compared to the average dog, and his metabolic rate is also comparatively low, meaning that he can have trouble getting the drugs out of his system. For this reason, you should always insist that your dog is weighed when dosages are being calculated, as some vets massively overestimate a Siberian Husky's weight due to his thick coat.

On the subject of vets, always chose one with decent emergency cover, preferably not a clinic miles away that would take too long to get to in a genuine emergency.

THE CURSE OF POPULARITY

Films like *Snow Dogs* and the corresponding rise in demand for

Siberians, have unfortunately led to them becoming one of the most popular breeds for puppy farmers and backyard breeders.

People can be bad breeders without qualifying for the term 'puppy farmer'. You will know a puppy farm when you see one. The dogs are kept in poor conditions and bred at every season to maximise profits. They are frequently unregistered or on another register, such as 'Dog Lovers', which means nothing. You cannot show a dog that is not registered with your national Kennel Club, or even race it with many clubs.

The KC registration does not guarantee a healthy, well-bred

puppy – a lot of puppy farmers register their stock because it is worth more that way – but at least you can ask the KC how many litters the breeder has registered, how many the mother of the litter has had, and whether the breeder has carried out any health tests. This is essential, as some puppy farmers have been caught falsifying pedigrees and health test certificates, and printing them out on their computers.

Puppy farmed puppies are usually unhealthy and unsocialised, and can have temperament problems due to their upbringing. If you insist on buying a pup from this source because he may be slightly cheaper than a well-bred puppy (and they are frequently not), you will probably find that it is a false economy, as you will spend more than you saved on the first of many visits to the vet. Buy pet insurance – you will need it!

Backyard breeders are harder to spot than puppy farmers. The dogs often look well cared for, and might even live in the house – or look as though they do. Some puppy farmers rotate their bitches into the houses of relatives when the litters are ready to be sold. At any rate, they will be more interested in your money than whether you will look after their puppy. If everybody refused to buy from these people, their market would disappear, and dogs would not be subjected to a miserable existence in the name of profit.

Bad signs to look out for:
- Advertising 'rare' coat or eye colours: These are unlikely to be rare at all, but they are a sign that looks are the selling point rather than health or temperament.
- Not health testing because their lines have never had any problems. The only reason why breeders do not health test their dogs is that it would cut into their profit margin.
- Selling puppies younger than 8 weeks (which can cause behavioural problems).
- Wanting to deliver the puppy to you, without you seeing the puppies' mother or the breeder's premises.
- Getting annoyed if you ask questions.
- Advertisements with mobile phone numbers only.
- Breeders who say they will send the papers on later.

In short, buying a puppy, especially off internet sites or from free papers, is a minefield. It is far better to have a good breeder recommended to you, and spend time getting to know them, their dogs and their set-up.

'DESIGNER' CROSSBREEDS
A huge number of people are now advertising husky crosses on the internet. Some of them, such as 'Huskamutes', are bred to satisfy people who think that huskies should be bigger than they are. Others claim to have bred out traits in a generation that took hundreds of years to fix in the breed! With a crossbreed, you never know how the dog will finish up. A German Shepherd Dog crossed with a Sibe, supposedly to increase his trainability, could be just as likely to grow up to be an odd-looking German Shepherd that runs away like a Sibe.

Almost all the advertisements claim that they are producing

When Olly, aged 14 weeks, came into breed rescue, he was on his fourth home. He was suffering from kennel cough, and nearly died from an infection he was carrying. He later developed cataracts in both eyes which required surgery. Fortunately, he had a happy ending, and is a much-loved member of a working team, but many puppy-farmed dogs are not as lucky.

The ideal home will focus on providing an outlet for the Siberian's energy and stamina.

healthier dogs. But, anecdotally, many of them seem to acquire the health problems of both parent breeds. It is possible that this is just because the type of people who are breeding these dogs are doing it purely for profit, and are using cheap, puppy farmed dogs, with no health checks, as their breeding stock. In spite of all this, amazingly, these crossbreeds are sometimes *more* expensive than pure-bred registered Sibes!

AN IDEAL HOME

A Siberian Husky can adapt to life in an urban environment, as long as he is given enough exercise – and that is a lot of exercise! In both town and country, this generally involves pounding the pavements for at least a couple of miles a day. Unless you find an

extremely well-fenced dog park, it is nearly impossible to find an enclosed space where you can allow your dog free-running exercise.

A lot of people get round this problem by buying horse-lunging reins so their husky can have a sense of freedom in unenclosed areas, yet still be safe. Flexi-leads are also good for this, but always make sure you buy the giant size – the webbing version, never the string one – and try not to let the dog yank it to the full extent to put a strain on the mechanism. If the lead gets wet, extend it fully to dry, and replace if it shows any signs of wear.

Mooching round the garden, however large, is no substitute for proper walks, especially for a Sibe. Many husky owners first got into

working their dogs because of the problems of giving them enough exercise. You can attach one dog with a specially made device to a mountain bike, or a purpose-made scooter. Then, when you get the almost inevitable second dog, it is safer to move up to a three-wheeled 'rig' with a bit more stability.

At this point you really need a decent mentor – your breeder may know someone in your area. Potentially good dogs can be ruined by bad training and lack of experience – even something as minor as being made to go down a hill too fast can make a dog nervous about running in future. More than anything, a sled dog needs to have confidence and trust in his owner/musher – and that trust needs to be earned.

THE FIRST SIBERIAN HUSKIES

Chapter 2

The origins of the Siberian Husky can be traced back thousands of years to the dogs developed by the Chukchi people of the Kolyma River basin in Northern Siberia. The dogs were used to haul the Chukchi hunters' catch of seals back from the coast to their settlements inland. They were selectively bred over many generations to be able to pull relatively light loads at moderate speeds over enormous distances. They had to withstand extremely low temperatures and be capable of working for a long time on comparatively small quantities of food.

Because of the lack of trees, the Chukchi sleds were made mostly of whalebone or driftwood washed up on the shores. The word Chukchi means 'rich in reindeer', so it is no great surprise that almost everything else was made from reindeer parts. The sleds were lashed together with rawhide from reindeer, and the loads rested on reindeer skins.

On open tundra where hidden crevasses and cliffs were a problem, the dogs would be attached to the sled in a fan hitch. This means that each dog is attached back to a single point on the sled with his own line, or trace. If a dog falls into a crevasse, he does not drag any other members of the team with him, and a single driver has more chance of being able to pull him back up than if three dogs, all on the same rope, had fallen down.

This arrangement requires a well-disciplined team, and is not so efficient for pulling heavy loads, so another method was developed where the dogs are harnessed either alternately or in pairs to a single gang line. This was obviously better for narrow trails through forests.

Only the best male dogs were left entire and bred on from to improve the pack. The rest were castrated to prevent arguments over bitches and make them easier to train. Castrated dogs also tend to hold their weight better on smaller amounts of food.

The Chukchi often took their dogs into their homes so, unlike some of the other sled dog breeds who lived outside constantly, it was very important that the Siberians had gentle and reliable temperaments. The nature of the Chukchi people was the reason why the Siberian Husky temperament is so good – they received much better treatment than most of the other arctic breeds, and repaid the tribe with affection. The Chukchi call themselves the 'Luoravetlan', which translates as the genuine or

The resemblance of the Siberian Husky (right) to the wolf (above) – when they are technically no more genetically related than a Chihuahua – can probably be explained by the fact that they developed in the same harsh environment as the wolf, so similar physical characteristics were of use to them.

real people. They believe that two huskies guard the gates to heaven and turn away anybody that has shown cruelty to dogs in their life. Sounds like a great idea…

RUSSIAN INFLUENCE

In the 1700s, the Russians tried to take over the lucrative fur trade, so they conquered or killed every other native Siberian tribe, except the Chukchi who kept outrunning them due to their dogs. They did, however, wipe out a regiment of Cossacks when backed into a corner.

Eventually, the Russians decided that actually conquering the tribe was far too much trouble, and just issued a proclamation claiming that they had. The tribe started to trade with the Russians, and there was an uneasy truce between the two parties for a long time.

However, with the coming of the Russian Revolution in 1917 when the Communists came to power, it was decreed that all traditional cultures that did not conform to their ideals should be wiped out. Many Chukchi and their dogs were killed, and the tribe also fell victim to diseases such as smallpox, which they had not previously been exposed to. The Communists attempted to reclassify native breeds of dog, and eventually issued the famous proclamation that stated that the Siberian Husky had never existed! In fact, by this time they were almost extinct in their own country. Fortunately, Siberian Huskies had long been sought

The Siberian Husky almost became extinct in its native land during the Russian Revolution.

after by people living on the other side of the Bering Strait for use in their fur trapping and gold mining industries, as well as for racing, so a sizeable population was safe over there.

THE GOLD RUSH

In the winter of 1898 the US economy was in crisis, and the fact that many people had nothing left to lose fuelled the desperation of the Gold Rush.

News spread that a trio known as the Three Lucky Swedes (even though one, Jafet Lindeberg, was a Norwegian) had discovered gold in a creek on the Seward peninsula, and many who had failed to strike it rich in the Klondike trailed along the frozen Yukon River in the hope of being luckier this time. A bustling town, called Nome, grew up to service the miners.

In winter, dog teams were the only practical method of travelling any distance. A good dog could be sold for a fortune, and dogs were even kidnapped from other parts of the country and shipped up to Alaska, as related in Jack London's classic book *The Call of the Wild*.

French Canadian fur trappers used the dogs to haul sledge loads of fur – the word 'mush' comes from the French word for 'go' – 'marche'.

Nobody is entirely sure when the first Siberians arrived in Alaska. The natives on the two sides of the Bering Strait often traded with each other, and these exchanges may have included dogs. However, the first recorded instance of Siberian Huskies being in the country was in 1909 when a team competed in a race called the All Alaska Sweepstakes.

THE SERUM RUN

If one single event was responsible for bringing the Siberian Husky to the attention of the general public, it was the Serum Run.

In 1925, there was an outbreak of diphtheria in Nome. Dr Curtis Welch was the only doctor in this part of the country, and his dwindling supply of serum was weak and out of date. Although diphtheria was a rare disease in the area, he had ordered serum in the summer, but it had not arrived and now the ports were iced in.

A supply was located in a hospital in Anchorage, and if transport could be found, it would arrive much quicker than getting supplies shipped from Seattle. Air travel in such cold

LEONHARD SEPPALA

Leonhard Seppala, a Norwegian born in Skibotn in 1877, emigrated to Alaska in 1900 to work in the gold fields for his friend and countryman, Jafet Lindeberg, one of the "three lucky Swedes".

In 1913, Lindeberg bought a team of Siberian Huskies, intended as a gift for the explorer Roald Amundsen, who was planning an expedition to the North Pole. He handed the young dogs over to Seppala to train. The expedition was cancelled with the outbreak of World War One, and Seppala was able to keep the dogs.

Scotty Allan encouraged Seppala to enter the 1914 All Alaska Sweepstakes, which was a nearly fatal mistake. The only experienced dog in his team was his leader, Suggen, who was half Siberian, half Malamute. In a blizzard Seppala lost the trail, and he was only saved by the good sense of Suggen, who managed to turn the team of young dogs away from a cliff at the last minute.

Seppala learned from his mistakes and returned to win the sweepstake in 1915, 1916 and 1917, as well as triumphing in many other races. For a while he seemed so invincible that some people thought he had special powers! However, his success was almost certainly down to the amazing relationship he had with his dogs.

temperatures was dangerous and experimental. The first ever winter flight in Alaska had only been made the year before, and the weather this time was a great deal worse. There were winds of up to 80 miles per hour – which was appalling even for Alaska. It was therefore decided to get the serum to the nearest station of Nenana by train, and transport it by dog team from there. It was 674 miles from Nenana to Nome, and the trip normally took the dog teams that delivered the mail 25 days. In an effort to speed up the trip, it was decided to use a relay system, with fresh dogs and drivers waiting at the roadhouses along the trail. At every stop the

serum had to be taken inside and warmed, as the glass containers could shatter if frozen.

The original plan was for Leonhard Seppala to take his best dogs and travel out of Nome to meet the relay at Nulato, approximately halfway between Nome and Nenana. He took 20 dogs, planning to drop some off at villages on the way out, so they would be fresh for the trip back. His lead dog was Togo, then 12 years old. Togo was the son of Suggen, Seppala's leader in his attempt on the 1914 All Alaska Sweepstakes, and Dolly, one of Jafet Lindeberg's original Siberians. Togo had not had a promising start to his career. He

was so badly behaved as a puppy that Seppala gave him away to a pet home. But Togo escaped and found his way back to the kennels, so Seppala let him stay. He turned out to be a natural born leader.

A good lead dog is truly priceless to a musher. A leader's intelligence and sixth sense for danger can mean the difference between life and death for the musher and the whole team. He has to be able to sniff out the trail beneath many layers of snow, and to detect when ice is unsafe to cross by feeling minute changes in the moisture levels through his paws. This ability was particularly important to Seppala, as the

Leonhard Seppala with Elizabeth Ricker.

THE ALL-ALASKA SWEEPSTAKES

This was the name given to the first properly organised, competitive long-distance sled dog race. In autumn 1907, the Nome Kennel Club was formed in the Board of Trade Saloon, with the official purpose of encouraging: "the breeding of superior dogs by holding races that would promote the greatest care in the future selection and breeding of Alaskan trail dogs".

There were many shorter races, but the main event was to be a race from Nome to Candle Creek and back again, a total distance of 408 miles. The course covered an area from the Arctic Ocean to the Bering Sea, and included an area charmingly called Death Valley. It was to be run in April so the weather would be less severe and the days longer, and the trail would still be as smooth as possible from a season's use.

The first race took place in 1908 to great public excitement – there was a three-day public holiday in Nome. The position of each team was telegraphed back to Nome, and people placed bets on the 10 entrants. The winner, John Hegness, recorded a time of 119 hours and 15 minutes, and won the $10,000 prize, but many times that amount were placed in bets on the event.

In 1909, a Russian fur trader named William Goosak, who had imported a team of dogs from Siberia, entered the All Alaska Sweepstakes. His team of Siberians were much smaller than the dogs in the other 11 teams, weighing in at only 40-50 pounds (18-22kg). The locals rather unkindly labelled them the 'Siberian Rats', and the odds were listed at 100 to 1 against them. Legend has it that the number of bets laid against them was so large that, if they had won, the Bank of Alaska would have gone bust.

Goosak hired a man called Louis Thrustrup to drive the team, and he may well have won if he had rested the dogs properly. As it was they came in third, much to everyone's surprise. Goosak won $1,000 and had to sell the team to Captain Charles Madsen to fund his trip home.

Also competing in this race was a young Scottish nobleman, Charles Fox Maule Ramsey (1885-1926), a younger son of the 13th Earl of Dalhousie. He was fascinated by the little dogs and chartered a boat so he could sail to Siberia. There he bought about 60 of the best racing dogs that the Chukchi had on offer at the Markovo Fair on the Anadyr River.

Ramsey entered three teams in the 1910 All Alaska Sweepstakes. The team driven by John 'Iron Man' Johnson came in first in a time of 74 hours, 14 minutes, and 37 seconds – this record time was never beaten until the race was restaged in 2008. Johnson had gone snow blind more than 100 miles from the finish line, and had to rely on his lead dog, Kolyma, to take him across Death Valley. Two of his 16 dogs finished the race riding on the sled. In order to ensure the welfare of the dogs, each team had to bring back all the dogs they started with, even if they were exhausted or injured.

The team Ramsey drove came in second, and his third team came in fourth. The third-place driver, AA 'Scotty' Allan, was from Scotland, so the first half of the field had a Scottish connection.

Scotty Allan and his team won the race in 1909, 1911 and 1912, and were in the top three a further six times. News of his outstanding ability reached the French Army, who asked for his help getting supplies and ammunition to units cut off in the Vosges Mountains during World War One. He bought hundreds of dogs, shipped them to France and taught the French soldiers to drive them. The dog teams also transported the wounded to hospitals, and the dog unit was awarded the French Croix De Guerre medal.

The All Alaska Sweepstakes was staged annually until 1917 when America entered World War One, and was not revived until 1983. When the race was restaged, Rick Swenson attempted to beat 'Iron Man' Johnson's record, but he took 10 hours longer over the same course. However, massively variable weather conditions mean that direct comparisons are impossible.

In 2008, the race was staged again, and this time Mitch Seavey, running Alaskan huskies, broke Johnson's record by nearly 13 hours. In fact, the first six mushers home all beat the 1910 record.

The highly competitive nature of the early sled dog races led to a massive improvement in the care of the dogs. Their diet was evaluated and enhanced, more care was taken of their feet, and some teams were even fitted with goggles to prevent snow blindness.

Dog teams were once the only viable method of transport in Alaskan winters.

Major Norman D. Vaughan, the first and last American to use a dog sled in the Antarctic, with one of the sleds used on the last expedition before dogs were banned for fear of carrying disease. In 1932 he drove a team from the Chinook Kennels in a demonstration event of sled dog racing at the Lake Placid Winter Olympics. In the Second World War he set up an Arctic Search and Rescue division, and rescued 26 air crew from the "Lost Squadron" off the Greenland ice sheet. He also competed in 13 Iditarods, completing six, starting at the rather advanced age of 72, and finishing his last one at the age of 84! In 1994, at the age of 88, Major Vaughan climbed the mountain that had been named after him by Admiral Byrd on his first expedition to the Ross Ice Shelf in 1928.

quickest route for his part of the relay was across the deadly sea ice of Norton Sound.

As the epidemic progressed, extra teams were added while the relay was already underway in order to speed it up. Unfortunately, Seppala could not be contacted to tell him to wait at Shaktoolik after he had crossed Norton Sound. By some miracle, the previous driver, Henry Ivanoff, found him on the trail, and Seppala set off with the serum for the return journey. He crossed Norton Sound for the second time that day, and when he pulled up on land to rest the dogs, they had travelled 84 miles in one day.

When he handed the serum over to Charlie Olson, the next driver, Seppala had driven 261 miles in total, including the hardest 91 miles of the relay, and he still had to travel back to Nome.

Gunnar Kaasen, a colleague of Seppala's, was meant to be the second-last driver in the relay. By the time the serum reached him at Bluff, a decision had been made to halt the relay for a few hours, as the weather was so extreme. Kaasen never received the message. He missed the Solomon roadhouse in the blizzard and, finding the next one at Port Safety in darkness because they assumed the relay had been halted, he

decided to do the last comparatively short stretch himself rather than waste time waking up the last driver and waiting for him to harness his team.

Kaasen arrived in Nome at 5.30am on 2 February. A trip that normally took 25 days had been accomplished in five and a half!

During the relay, newspapers all over the United States had given daily updates on its progress, and afterwards public demand for continued coverage of the event was huge. Appeals raised money for the drivers, most of whom were native Athabaskan Indians or Eskimos.

Gunnar Kaasen was persuaded

to go on a tour round the United States. A producer named Sol Lesser bought the team and made a short film called *Balto's Race to Nome*. Money was raised to put up a bronze statue of Balto in Central Park, New York, sculpted by Frederick Roth. The inscription on the statue reads:

Dedicated to the indomitable spirit of the sled dogs that relayed anti-toxin six hundred miles over rough ice, across treacherous waters, through arctic blizzards from Nenana to the relief of a stricken Nome in the winter of 1925.
Enurance, Fidelity, Intelligence.

Then Kaasen had to leave the dogs and go back to his job delivering supplies in Alaska. Some people were jealous of the attention Kaasen had received, and even accused him of missing the last stop on the relay on purpose. Even Seppala was annoyed that Balto had got all the press attention rather than Togo, who had done a much more difficult stretch of the run. The situation had not been helped by the fact that Togo had run off after some reindeer with a team-mate, and was not around in the immediate aftermath of the relay.

Balto and his team were sold on to a promoter, and ended up neglected in a sideshow. A Cleveland businessman, named George Kimble, saw them and started a campaign with his local newspaper, the *Cleveland Plain Dealer*, to raise the money to rescue them. In 10 days they had the $2,000 required, and the

dogs lived out their days as a popular attraction at a zoo in Cleveland, Ohio.

In 1975 there was a 50th anniversary re-enactment of the Serum Run involving many of the sons and grandsons of the original drivers. They took six days longer to complete the route.

OUT OF ALASKA

In 1926, Seppala took 43 dogs, including Togo, on his own tour of America. They regularly drew massive crowds that required police control. Polar explorer Roald Amundsen, who would have taken Seppala's first Siberians to the North Pole if not for the outbreak of World War One, gave Togo a gold medal at Madison Square Gardens.

After the tour, Seppala was invited to compete in the sled dog races in New England by

Arthur Walden, who had helped organise the first race there in 1921. Walden's own dogs, the huge tawny coloured Chinooks, bred from the McKenzie River Husky, had been as unbeatable there as Seppala's Siberians had been in Alaska, and he wanted to test the two breeds against each other.

At his first race in Poland Springs in Maine in January 1927, Seppala beat the other competitors by quite a way, in spite of his dogs being out of condition from the tour, and the fact that he stopped to help another musher on the way round.

That other driver was Elizabeth Ricker, who was so impressed with the little Siberians that she and Seppala formed a partnership at her kennels in Poland Springs. They bred from

Lorna Barnes Taylor (later Demidoff) around 1935. All these dogs are from one litter whelped in 1932, and include Ch. Togo of Alyeska, and Lorna's foundation bitch Tosca of Alyeska.

his existing dogs, and brought in more from Siberia. The last were brought out in 1930, before the Communists prevented the export of any more. Olaf Swenson, an explorer and fur trader from Michigan, brought these last dogs out, buying some for $150. Kreevanka and Tserko from this group went to Liz Ricker, then later to Harry Wheeler. Seppala and Ricker were instrumental in helping to get the Siberian recognised as a breed by the American Kennel Club.

In 1932, after a whirlwind romance, Liz Ricker married the explorer Kaare Nansen, the son of fellow explorer Fridtjof Nansen, a member of whose 1888 expeditionary team Balto had been named after! Her partnership with Seppala was dissolved, and the dogs were sold to Harry Wheeler of the Gatineau kennels in St Jovite, Canada. Wheeler used the suffix 'Seppala' and continued to breed and race the dogs.

These dogs were the basis of most of the early Siberian kennels, including Chinook, Lorna Demidoff's Monadnock, and Cold River, owned by Marie Frothingham. Bill Shearer, a very successful sled dog racer who ran

Eva 'Short' Seeley and Ch. Wonalancet's Baldy of Alyeska, after becoming the first husky to win a Working Group, which he did at the North Shore Kennel Club in 1941.

the Foxstand kennels in New Hampshire, also used many Seppala dogs in his breeding programme.

In 1950, JD McFaul of Quebec, who had been breeding mainly Seppala dogs under the Gatineau affix, bought out Wheeler's kennels and started using the Seppala suffix. In 1963, the dogs were sold to Earl and Natalie Norris of Alaskan kennels, who took them home to Alaska.

INTO THE RING
The Siberian Husky was first recognised as a breed by the American Kennel Club in 1930, and in Canada in 1939. The

Breed Standard was published in 1932.

The first Siberian to appear in the AKC Stud Book in December 1930 was a bitch bred by Julien Hurley of the Northern Light kennel in Alaska, called Fairbanks Princess Chena. The January 1931 issue listed 21 dogs, all from the Northern Light kennel, and a total of 69 appeared in the Stud Book that year.

The first Siberian bench Champion in America was made up in July 1932 – Ch. Northern Light Kobuck, owned by Oliver Shattuck and bred by Julien Hurley. It was four years before the next Champion was made up in 1936. Ch. Shankhassack Lobo was bred by the Seeleys and owned by Professor Charles Floyd Jackson, who became the first president of the Siberian Husky Club of America when it was formed in 1938. He was sired by Sepp III, who Seppala said was a son of Togo, out of Tosca of Alyeska, before she was sold to Lorna Demidoff. Lobo's photograph was used as the Breed Standard picture in the 1935 and 1938 editions of the *AKC Complete Dog Book*. His sister, Ch. Cheenah of Alyeska, became the third American Champion in

Lorna Demidoff running a team in Fitzwilliam, New Hampshire, in the late 1940s.

Lorna Demidoff and her show team winning at The National Capital Show in 1960.

1938. The first bitch to be made up, she was also the first owned by Milton and Eva (known as 'Short') Seeley.

EARLY SIBERIAN KENNELS

NORTHERN LIGHT
In spite of having been instrumental in securing recognition for the breed and establishing the original Breed Standard, Julien Hurley mostly concentrated on racing, and did not register any dogs after 1933. Only a few descendants of his dogs remain in Anadyr lines.

CHINOOK
Arthur Walden, who had invited Seppala to New England, bred his large Chinook dogs at a kennel by the name of Wonalancet, where it was based. When he became the dog handler on Admiral Byrd's

first Antarctic expedition, he went into partnership with Milton and Eva Seeley, and they ran the kennels in his absence. The Seeleys bred huskies under the Alyeska affix, their first one being a granddaughter of Seppala's Togo, called Tanta of Alyeska. When Walden returned and sold them the rest of the business, they changed the kennel name to Chinook after Walden's famous lead dog, but pretty much abandoned the breed named after him.

They continued to train huskies for Byrd's expeditions. For Operation High Jump, a mission to set up an Antarctic research base, Milton chose 50 Siberians instead of the larger dogs more usually chosen for such work. The explorers reported that not only were the Sibes far faster than the Malamutes and Eskimo dogs, but

were also far easier to feed.

They also provided many of the search and rescue dog teams used in World War Two.

MONADNOCK
Moseley Taylor, the publisher of the *Boston Globe*, bought a puppy called Togo of Alyeska from the Seeleys, along with six others as a team for his wife, Lorna, to race. Lorna started showing simply "to have something to do with the dogs in the summer". In 1939, she made Togo up as her first Champion. Great grandson of Seppala's Togo, he was also a great lead dog, with whom she won many races.

In 1941, after divorcing Taylor, she married the Russian Prince, Nikolai Lapouchine-Demidoff, and was known as the Princess from then on.

Lorna bought her foundation

Millie Turner, daughter of Marie Frothingham, and the Cold River team.

bitch, Tosca of Alyeska, from the Seeleys, and her first home-bred Champion was Ch. Panda of Monadnock in 1941.

Later, Panda's descendent, Monadnock's Pando, became the most influential stud in the breed, and started the fashion for black and white, blue-eyed huskies. In the 1960s, Pando and his offspring dominated the US show scene. He won five consecutive Best of Breed awards at Westminster Show, and his son, Monadnock's King, was the first Siberian to win Best in Show in America outside Alaska.

Lorna continued to run dogs for pleasure well into her sixties.

COLD RIVER
Starting her kennel with mainly Northern Light dogs, then Wheeler ones, Mrs Marie Frothingham, known affectionately as 'the Duchess', did not really show her dogs, concentrating instead on racing. She did, however, breed several Champions, including Dr Lombard's famous leader, Ch. Helen of Cold River. On her retirement, she passed many of her best dogs on to the man who had driven her teams for her, Lyle Grant, who, with his wife, Marguerite, went on to set up the Marlytuk kennel.

ALASKAN'S/ANADYR
In 1935, Earl Norris started up the Alaskan kennels in Idaho, a state where people were used to racing hound types and setters. He later bought his first AKC registered Siberian from Northern

Light and moved to Alaska.

He saw the young Natalie Jubin on the cover of the *New York Herald Tribune* and wrote to her. Natalie arrived in Alaska with two dogs from the Chinook kennels. This included Chinook's Alladin of Alyeska, who became the foundation stud for the young couple's breeding programme, based on the best working dogs of US and Canadian kennels.

Earl helped start or revive many sled dog races when interest in the sport had declined. In 1949 he and Natalie helped set up the Alaska Kennel Club, and three years later, the Siberian Husky Club of Alaska. In 1956, this club held the first independent Siberian Speciality show where AKC Championship points could be won. It attracted 35 entries, which, at that time, was the largest gathering of Siberians at any AKC show.

The Norris's dogs were very successful in the show ring. Their lead dog, Ch. Bonzo of Anadyr CD, Alladin's grandson, became the first ever Siberian to win BIS at an AKC All Breeds show at Fairbanks in 1955. Bonzo was also their main leader from 1954-60, finishing in the top five teams of the Fur Rondy race for seven years. As Earl said, "We show our race dogs, others race show dogs." It takes real skill to breed successfully for both pastimes.

The Alaskan's Anadyr kennels exported stock all over the world, providing foundation dogs for many other famous kennels.

THE IDITAROD

In the late 1960s, mushing as a sport was beginning to die out. Historian Dorothy Page and sled dog driver Joe Redington organised a race with a $25,000 prize to stimulate interest. Run in 1967, it was called the Centennial Iditarod Sled Dog Race, to commemorate the 100th anniversary of the purchase of Alaska, and was only 27 miles long.

In 1973, the race was increased to 1,049 miles, following the trail from Anchorage to Nome. Because the trails are now prepared in advance using snowmobiles, the race is usually over in around 10 days, rather than the three weeks it used to take to cover the distance.

For the safety of the dogs, teams must compete in two qualifying races within the previous two years. These are all over 500 miles long. There are also veterinary examinations at each checkpoint, and the vet can insist that any dog that is sick or tired is dropped from the race.

There is a large entry fee, and this does not cover essentials, such as food and straw for the dogs, which has to be flown in and dropped at the 26 checkpoints of the race.

CROSSING THE POND

The first pair of Siberians were imported into Britain in 1968 by Mr and Mrs Proffitt, who had seen them on holiday in Europe. Two eight-week-old puppies came in from Norway – a bitch called Togli and a dog called Killick from Alaskan/Anadyr lines.

Commander William Cracknell brought in the second pair after he was posted to the UK by the US Navy in 1969. Yeso-Pac's Tasha was the granddaughter of both the famous Ch. Monadnock's Pando and Ch. Alyeska's Suggen of Chinook. Savdajaure's Samovar was also from Monadnock lines, and the son of two US Champions. Tasha spent six months in quarantine, while Sam had to endure a stay of 11 months, because of a rabies scare.

In 1970, Don and Liz Leich returned from America, with their three daughters, and the third pair of Siberians to enter the country.

They had purchased an unrelated pair from two different breeders in America, and registered them as Ilya and Douschka of Northwood – Don's middle name, and their original choice of affix.

Ilya was mostly Monadnock lines, while Doushka was part Monadnock, part Canadian working lines.

When Commander Cracknell contacted the British Kennel Club to register the dogs, they wanted him to register them as 'Husky', which was the name used at the time for the breed later known as the Eskimo Dog. Husky is a generic name for all sled-dog breeds, first used in the 19th century, and is a corruption of the word Eskimo. Commander Cracknell insisted that they were registered as a separate breed, arguing that they should be registered as 'Siberian Huskies' as they were in America, and eventually the KC agreed.

In May 1971, Commander

Liz Leich, who imported some of the first Siberian Huskies to Britain, and who did so much to establish the breed.

Ilya and Douschka of Northwood, the pups brought back from America by the Leich family.

Cracknell bred and registered the first ever British litter of Siberians with the KC, under his Micnicroc's affix. Tasha and Sam had seven puppies, effectively more than doubling the population of Siberians in Britain overnight!

The second litter in the country was from the same parents, and the third was born in May 1972 – the first litter for the influential Forstal's kennel. These five puppies were from Samovar and Douschka, and included Forstal's Sernik, the first red and white Siberian to appear in Britain.

SIBERIAN BREED CLUB

In 1976, the Husky Club of Great Britain got the KC to change their breed name from 'Husky' to 'Eskimo Dog', and the Siberian owners who had previously been catered for by this club formed a club of their own.

The Siberian Husky Club of Great Britain was formed in May 1977 with the aim of educating people about the breed, and promoting a functional, dual-purpose Siberian. Later it was instrumental in organising health-testing schemes for hereditary conditions, such as glaucoma and hip dysplasia. Today the club organises shows and holds rallies for all KC-registered sled dogs. It also runs the Dual Championship awards based on combined points awarded at shows and rallies.

EARLY SHOWING IN THE UK

Originally, Siberians could only be shown in 'Any Variety Rare Breeds', 'Any Variety Sled Dog', or 'Any Variety Not Separately Classified' classes. Gradually, during the 1970s and early 1980s, the breed was given more

of their own classes at shows as their numbers steadily increased. In 1986, Siberians were finally awarded eight sets of Championship Certificates. The first CCs were appropriately awarded by Sally Leich, whose family was so instrumental in introducing the breed to Britain.

The first British Champion was Ch. Forstals Mikishar the Amarok. Miki was the son of Forstals Kassan, who was from the Leichs' original pair, Ilya and Douschka, and Micnicroc's Nanushka from Commander Cracknell's first litter.

By the time CCs were available, Miki was 10 years old. He came out of retirement long enough to get his three CCs; the final one was awarded in August 1986, at WKC, just before his 11th birthday. He sired three Champions and lived to 17 years

Mikalya's Nadine (Ch. Forstal Mikishar the Amarok x Mikris Natalya). This photo was used by the Kennel Club as the Breed Standard picture for several years in the 80s and early 90s.

and 7 months old.

At the same show where Miki was made up, Forstals Noushka became the first female British Champion.

HITTING THE TRAIL

Sally Leich quickly decided that the best way to exercise the Forstal Siberians was in the way for which they had been designed, and worked them – in spite of the opinion, prevalent at the time, that it was impossible to work sled dogs in the UK.

The first working event in the UK was a 20-mile sponsored run for Siberian Welfare on the South Downs Way. There were two teams of eight dogs, driven by Sally Leich and Sandra Bayliss, each with a passenger.

The first sled-dog race in the UK was held in October 1978, on Ministry of Defence land at

Hankley Common in Surrey. The trail for this was only three miles long. Getting trails of decent distances for both training and rallies continues to be a problem in Britain, partly for reasons of access, but also due to high temperatures and humidity.

Early rigs were enormous, weighing 100 lbs (45kg) or more, but lightweight models were quickly developed, and this resulted in the opportunity for two-dog classes, which opened up the sport to people without the facilities for keeping large numbers of dogs. These days, scooter and bike classes mean you can start working with only one dog. The design of British rigs has continued to evolve until they are now so sophisticated and competitive that they are exported overseas.

There are now several

organisations that put on races, as well as the Siberian Husky Club. These include British Siberian Husky Racing Association, Affiliated British Sleddog Activities, Sled Dog Association of Scotland, Scottish Siberian Husky Club and Alaskan Malamute Working Association. Many of these have different rules and eligibility criteria for types or breeds of dog, which is where a good mentor and a bit of research on their websites comes in handy, preferably before you buy your dog. It would be annoying to find that all the races in your area are run by an organisation you cannot race with because you bought an unregistered dog.

It is rare to get the opportunity to race on sleds in the UK, but in 1983 the first British rally on snow was held at Glen Esk, on land belonging to the Earl of Dalhousie.

Goosak of Kolyma. Imported from Holland in 1980 by the Leich family, Goosak was one of the most influential sires in the breed.

Ali Koops with Ch. Forstal Meshka and some of his trophies. He was the 7th British Champion in the breed, and won 13 CCs and 3 RCCs. He is still the only Siberian to win Best in Show at an all-breeds Championship show, and was runner up in the Working Group at Crufts, in the days when that group included all today's Pastoral breeds as well.

Ch. Aceca's American Pie, known as Spot The Dog, was awarded 18 CCs, 12 BOBs and 10 RCCs, coming out of retirement to win his last ticket at Crufts at the age of 11. He also won the SHCGB Dual Championship in 1996 and 1997.

Left: Early rigs were enormous and required large teams to pull them. Right: These two leaders led their race team for three consecutive seasons.

Patron at that time of the Siberian Husky Club of Great Britain, the Earl was the nephew of Charles Fox Maule Ramsey, who originally helped bring the Siberian to America.

The first Aviemore rally, now the biggest event in the UK working calendar, regularly attracting over 200 entries, was held the following year. It almost had to be cancelled due to the snow blocking roads. Out of 20 entries, only 12 managed to get to Aviemore. Most of these had abandoned their cars at Blair Atholl, and got on a train with dozens of dogs – much to the bewilderment of local commuters.

There have been a limited number of snow rallies in most parts of the UK since then, but as lack of the white stuff has always been a problem in Britain, we are perhaps more advanced in the development of a 'dryland' racing culture than some other countries where recent lack of snow cover is forcing them to start using rigs to extend their season. Although frankly, in a British winter, the term 'dryland' can be somewhat inaccurate...

THE CURRENT SCENE

In the United States, the popularity of the Siberian Husky as a breed has decreased since its high point in the 80s. This is probably due to people having less space, and less time to devote to such an energetic dog. New zoning laws also restrict the number of dogs on a property in many places.

Many Siberians in America are purebred, though registered not with the American Kennel Club but with one of the many profit-making registry companies that simply act as a list and print out a pedigree for a fee. The AKC is the only major registry that has health requirements. It has DNA testing for dogs that produce a certain number of litters, and – apart from the United KC – it is the only organisation to hold conformation shows and other canine sporting events.

Entries at shows are dropping in general, and it is not unusual for the Siberian entry at a Championship show to be in single figures. In such a large country, the distances to drive to shows have always been considerable, but it is only recently that the rising cost of fuel has made dog showing a prohibitively expensive hobby for many.

In the world of competitive dog racing, the Siberian Husky has mostly been replaced by the Alaskan Husky, a dog constructed

In Britain, the majority of the dogs in the show ring are also working dogs. Here Ch. Rajarani Sashenka leads her team at the Greystoke Rally, weeks before winning the Bitch CC at Crufts.

by the addition of faster breeds, such as Pointers and hounds. However, it has been suggested that if artificial aids, such as coats and boots, for the short-coated dogs were banned, the Siberian's natural suitability for the job would see it make a comeback.

In any case, some people will always prefer the beauty and character of the Siberian, and purebred racing is still popular, mainly concentrated in the areas that get the most reliable snow cover.

Although the majority of American show Siberians are not

worked, for those that are, the AKC has recently recognised the Siberian Husky Club of America's Sled Dog Degree programme. Dogs are awarded the titles SD: Sled Dog; SDX: Sled Dog Excellent; or SDO: Sled Dog Outstanding, according to a system based on how many miles they have completed in harness.

Dryland racing has started to become more popular in America, both to extend the season and to allow the spread of the sport into new areas. Changing weather patterns have also meant that traditional

racing areas have been less able to rely on regular snow at the right times.

For a breed that has only been in the UK for around 40 years, it has not taken long for the popularity of Sibes to reach critical levels. The internet has been a gift for puppy farmers and backyard breeders who care more for their profits than the puppies they breed or the people that buy them. Many people seem to do less research into a dog that could live for 15 years than they would into buying a new mobile phone.

The combination of

Five Champions from Chris McRae's Zoox kennel: Ch. Zateizzi Chleo Surprise at Zoox JW, Ch. Zateizzi Realy a Zoox, Ch. Zateizzi Chleozha by Zoox, Ch. Zoox Prinmore Pride JW, and Ch. Zoox Seven of Nine.

irresponsible breeders and uninformed buyers, alongside the fact that owning Siberians takes rather more effort than many other breeds, has meant that the rescue schemes are overflowing.

The Kennel Club is making some efforts to increase health testing, but many more unregistered than registered pups are produced, and so it is impossible to keep a check on the breed in general.

Entries at shows are dropping in Britain, too, although a poor entry at a Championship show would still be around 40-50

dogs. While rising fuel and entry costs have played a part in this, another reason is that Britain is one of the few countries that has attempted to avoid the split between show and working dogs seen in other countries. Most of the Siberians in the British show ring are the same dogs that are regularly worked, but an increasing number of judges are all-rounders brought in to judge several breeds and they have no experience of what makes a sound working dog. They tend to go for less athletic dogs with a flashy gait that would make them

poor workers who would tire easily.

To ensure the dual-purpose nature of the breed is maintained, it is vital that good, standard-fitting working dogs are kept in the show ring.

Rally entries are down slightly, but the sport remains buoyant. Breed club events restricted to purebred registered sled dogs can get 60-100 teams, with Aviemore fielding over 200. Most racing in Britain is for purebred sled-dog breeds, with a few clubs holding open classes for unregistered dogs and other breeds.

A SIBERIAN HUSKY FOR YOUR LIFESTYLE

Chapter 3

The decision to invite a Siberian Husky into your life should not be taken lightly. Puppies of any breed are adorable; husky puppies are irresistibly gorgeous and their good looks and winning ways mean your heart can often win out over your head. The sweet, little, teddy bear puppy you brought home will soon be doing a wall of death around your living room furniture, will chew your remote/mobile phone/MP3 player and will raid your bins – albeit with some considerable charm! Lock up your valuables in the early months and even later. Ornaments or objects that might be ignored for weeks, or even months, can be targeted out of the blue and reduced to smithereens in the blink of an eye. A Siberian Husky is not for the house proud.

WHAT DOES A SIBERIAN HUSKY NEED?

Although a working, hardy breed, a Siberian Husky is also a pack animal and needs company – that is going to be you, especially if you have no other dogs. A lone husky left in an outdoor kennel for hours on end, with little to do, is a sorry sight. A solo husky left alone in the garden without interaction will uproot your prize dahlias (or any other flowers or shrubs for that matter), dig holes in your lawn until it looks like the ideal set for a re-enactment of the battle of the Somme, and may howl mournfully until the neighbours complain. A home-alone Siberian with an unfenced garden and nothing to do will probably escape, cause traffic accidents, chase cats and hunt small livestock. Once your husky has got a taste for this, you will have to fence your house as if it were Colditz Castle to prevent your canine Houdini from escaping.

As a Siberian Husky grows older, he will need plenty of stimulation and exercise to become a well-balanced, acceptable member of the household. An under-stimulated husky is an unhappy husky, and one that can get himself into all sorts of fixes. That said, a well-trained, well-exercised dog, who is often engaged with, is a delightful companion and will make you wonder why you even considered another breed.

So be honest with what you can do for your new dog. A Siberian can live for up to 13 or 14 years, so you may want to look at your lifestyle now and in the future before taking the Siberian Husky road. If you are a

Although the breed enjoys a good run, you should only ever let them off a lead in a very well-fenced area.

self-confessed couch potato, a husky may not be the obvious choice for you – unless you are prepared to pay someone else to do the work for you. On the other hand, if you are a fit, active, outdoors sort of person, who enjoys physical exercise and has an indifference to bad weather, a husky may be just the dog for you.

Rehoming charities state that a dog should not be left alone for more than four hours, which seems a sensible idea not just because he needs company, but because he may get into trouble or become ill. Leaving a dog for the duration of a working day – eight hours or more – represents a long time without attention, and boredom will result in an unhappy and potentially destructive dog.

EXERCISE
Before committing to this lovely breed, have an honest look at your lifestyle. There is nothing a husky loves more than exercise, so make sure your work schedule means that you can take your Siberian out at least three times a day – more if you can manage it! Siberians are bred to run and have high levels of activity, so ensure you are prepared to give them the necessary exercise.

An adult husky does not need to be part of a mushing team to get his exercise, but he needs lots of walks in different places and some running, at least once a day, in a safe area. There are various activities you can do with your husky to ensure he gets plenty of running exercise once he has matured at between 12 and 18 months.

TRAINING
An untrained, under-stimulated Siberian Husky can be an unmanageable nightmare, and is often the reason why Siberians aged between 8 and 18 months end up in rescue. Generally, the dog in this situation has not received the training, stimulation or exercise that he needs in order to become the well-balanced pet that a husky can be.

For more information, see Chapter Six: Training and Socialisation.

FINANCIAL COMMITMENT
As well as working out if you have time for a Siberian Husky, you also need to work out if you can afford to keep him.
- **Food:** Your puppy will need a high-quality diet to thrive, pre-prepared or otherwise, and neither is a cheap proposition.

- **Training:** A course of puppy classes, and, perhaps, further training classes throughout your dog's life.
- **Preventative health care:** You will need to follow a vaccination programme recommended by your vet, plius regular flea and worming treatments. These all add up.
- **Neutering:** You may wish to get your husky neutered, so you will need to factor in the cost of this.
- **Vet's bills:** Most huskies are quite low-maintenance but they can get into scrapes, requiring veterinary care. Pet insurance or money set aside for such eventualities will soften the blow of veterinary bills. Bear in mind that older dogs will need more care and may require more regular visits to the vet.
- **Equipment:** Dog toys, dog accessories and dog beds will also be needed.
- **Holidays:** If you cannot take your Siberian Husky when you go on vacation, you will need to find reputable boarding kennels. Other alternatives, which are usually preferable but often more costly, are employing someone to board your dog in their home or getting a dog sitter to mind your dog 24/7 while you are sunning yourself on the beach!

Again, you need to ensure that the dog boarder or dog sitter has the necessary experience, qualifications, expertise and knowledge to cope with your pet in these situations, which may come at a price.

Siberians are not a breed that will be happy left to their own devices all day. They need mental stimulation and company – either yours or that of another dog.

DO YOUR HOMEWORK

You may think you have done sufficient research if you have read books on the breed or found information on the internet, but nothing can beat seeing Siberians in the flesh and learning what they are like to live with at first hand.

The ideal place to do this is at dog shows and husky rallies. Seeing a lot of huskies together, and watching them interact, will give you a good idea of whether this is the dog for you. Talking to people at dog shows and rallies will also give you a real insight into husky traits that may not ultimately appeal to you. Most husky owners are very honest about the ups and downs of husky ownership, so you will normally get a warts-and-all picture.

If you are set on the Siberian Husky, shows and rallies are a good place to discover where the good breeders can be found and if any of them have litters or are planning litters of puppies.

MALE OR FEMALE?

Before you contact a breeder, try to work out if you would be better suited to owing a male or a female.

If you have a bitch and do not spay her, she will generally have two seasons a year, during which time she may not be as keen to work for a few weeks, she may go off her food and seem moody, becoming by turns quiet or playful, skittish and distracted.

She may be less tolerant of other bitches. Post-season some female huskies suffer with phantom pregnancy-type symptoms, becoming more protective of resources such as food and beds, and this should be taken into consideration if you have other dogs in the household.

Females can live quite happily together for most of the year, but this is a time when fights can break out – and they can be bloody, serious affairs. During this period it will be necessary to minimise opportunities for disagreements by not leaving food around and by ensuring dogs have plenty of space and enough exercise to minimise frustration. General opinions of bitches are that Sibe females are more aloof

Bills at the vet can mount up so it is advisable to get pet insurance, especially if you don't know the full health history of your puppy's parents.

and independent than males. This will vary from dog to dog and personalities of the individual dogs should be taken into account.

Male huskies are deemed a little easier and less hormonal, but they are generally bigger and stronger, so your own size, strength and requirements should be taken into consideration when choosing the sex of your new exciting companion. Males are generally deemed to be more affectionate and attentive. Entire males (and often those who have been castrated) will tend to scent mark with urine, two males will mark more, so the house-proud should beware. Males can live quite happily together; though squabbles between males can occur, they are generally less serious than those between females and are hopefully short-lived affairs.

If you are not planning to breed from your male or female Siberian then neutering is certainly an option and, done early enough, you may be able to avoid some sexually-related behaviours as well as certain cancers and conditions (such as the potentially fatal 'pyometra' or womb infection) later in life.

For more information, on neutering, see Chapter Five: The Best of Care.

COLOUR

The fun of Siberian Husky puppies is that any colour is acceptable. Huskies can range from pure white, to varying shades of grey and white, through

The male is usually bigger and stronger than the female, but often easier to live with.

to black and white. They can be red and white, brown and white, or cream. Solid colours and piebalds (with spots and splodges) are also acceptable. Anything really does go!

Huskies may have the characteristic facial mask that you often see in classic Siberian Husky photos or they may be one solid colour without a mask, known as a 'dirty face' if it is a dark colour with little white.

Eyes can be various shades of brown or blue, or one eye can be blue and one brown in the same dog. Some eyes may be particoloured.

COAT COLOURS

The Siberian Husky comes in absolutely any colour, or combination of colours and markings. This leads to some really striking coat colours and patterns.

THE EYES HAVE IT

Eyes can be any shade of blue or brown, or one of each, which is called bi-eyed. Siberian eyes can also be parti-coloured, which means that the blue and the brown colour appear in the same eye.

Brown eyes.

Blue eyes.

Bi-eyed.

Parti-coloured.

FINDING A BREEDER

If you decide to take the plunge into husky ownership, the next step is to need to find a reputable breeder that has, preferably, been recommended by somebody you trust, or by one of the Siberian Husky breed clubs who will be familiar with careful breeders producing happy, healthy huskies.

A good breeder is somebody who has tested the dam (mother) and has sought to minimise the possibility of breeding from unhealthy stock. Normal tests will include hip scoring, and eye tests for cataracts, glaucoma and other eye defects (see Chapter Eight: Happy and Healthy). The owners of the bitch will have searched for

the best complementary match for the mating – not a dog that just happens to live down the road – and the sire (father) will similarly have undergone the same health examinations. A good breeder will ensure that both dogs have sound personalities and conform to the Breed Standard (see Chapter

A responsible breeder will have carried out health checks on breeding stock.

Seven: The Perfect Siberian Husky) to ensure, as far as possible, that the offspring are hearty and healthy. A well-put-together husky will generally be a healthy husky and this will, hopefully, protect you from heartache and costly veterinary bills for illnesses that could have been prevented, such as hip dysplasia and blindness due to cataracts or glaucoma.

A responsible breeder will ensure that the mother and puppies have been brought up within the home rather than a barn or an outside kennel. If very young puppies are exposed to the hustle and bustle of everyday home life early on, it will help to prevent fear problems as the puppy matures.

A knowledgeable breeder will make sure that you are able to provide the right home for a Siberian Husky, and will ask you to sign a declaration, stating that if, at any time, you are unable to continue caring for your dog, you will return him to the breeder in the first instance. This, above all things, will tell you that the breeder is a caring husky owner who is doing the best for their dogs. It also means that if your circumstances were to change dramatically, your dog would have a place to go. A good breeder will be happy to answer any questions you might have, and be keen for you to contact them in the future with queries you may have about your husky. In my experience, the breeder of your puppy often becomes a lifelong friend.

VIEWING THE LITTER

Once you have found a good breeder and the pups have been born, you should be able to visit the litter. Breeders should be happy to let you visit before you come to pick up your puppy. Puppies at five weeks of age are just getting interesting, and you will get a good impression of what your puppy might be like.

The breeder will have pick of the litter if they are planning to keep a pup, and some of the other pups may already be allocated. This means you may not have a full choice and the breeder will probably help you to select a suitable puppy. Obviously, you can walk away if you are not happy with this concept, although turning your back on a cute litter of husky puppies is not for the faint-hearted.

Hopefully, the breeder will have ensured that the nest area is separate from the toileting area, and has not left the puppies for extended periods of time to roll around in urine and faeces, as this could have implications for toilet training when your puppy comes to you. A good breeder will make sure that the puppies have access to different toys and safe objects so that they have plenty of stimulation and can get used to different sensations, surfaces and novelties. This will mean that your puppy is better able to adjust to new situations, and will take moving to a new home in his stride.

Most Siberian Husky mothers are careful but should be happy for visitors to view their offspring. In the presence of the breeder, a mother should allow you to stroke and play with her puppies whilst keeping a weather eye on the situation. Overly possessive behaviour should be viewed with caution, as such traits can be passed to the puppies. In my experience, it is usually best to make a fuss of the mother first and

spend a little time getting to know her before diving in and cuddling her puppies. Check first with the breeder as to how they would prefer you to behave. Be calm, gentle and reassuring and be guided by the bitch's owner. Avoid breeders who will not allow you to see the bitch with her puppies, as this could indicate a problem.

In most cases, the stud dog – the father of the puppies – will not be living on the premises. However, you can observe the mother, which will give you a good idea of some of the traits she may pass on to her pups. A puppy will also learn a great deal of behaviour from his mother,

Puppies should be outgoing and sociable, even with strangers.

and from his siblings, so it is vital that she is a sound dog.

You may also get the opportunity to see some close relatives, such as previous offspring still with the breeder, cousins, aunts and uncles. They will usually be related in some shape or form to your puppy (your breeder will be happy to tell you), and they may all give a clue to what you can expect from your new husky. You can be reassured if your puppy's relatives are friendly, easy-going, confident and without health problems.

When you go to see a litter, look out for the following signs, which indicate that the puppies are well reared and healthy:

• Depending on when you visit, the puppies should be lively and ready to come up to greet you. Puppies do sleep a lot of the time, so if your visit coincides with a time when they are resting, you might like to arrange a second visit to ensure this is not a sign of lethargy or ill health.

• The puppies should be clean with healthy-looking coats and their eyes, nose and ears should be clear with no sign of discharge that might indicate some sort of problem or infection.

• Check to see their bottoms are clean, and that they are not suffering from diarrhoea, which might suggest a tummy bug or something more serious.

Nurture your puppy's strengths and you could end up with a top-class working dog. This puppy is now running in harness on a winning team.

CHOOSING A PUPPY

It is important to be honest with the breeder about the hopes and plans you have for your Siberian Husky, as this will help them select a puppy that is most likely to suit your lifestyle. The breeder will have spent many hours watching the litter, and will know the puppies' individual personalities.

Regardless of whether you are looking for a show dog, a working dog or simply a pet, your criteria should be that your puppy is healthy, well socialised, confident and happy. The breeder will have undertaken all the appropriate health checks on the parents to ensure the best possible start for your new best friend.

SHOW DOG

If you are keen to show your Siberian Husky, you will already be aware of lines of huskies that have had recent or past success in the show ring. This will give you a good head start. Confident puppies, with a touch of showmanship, are more likely to have the presence to progress in a show career, whereas nervous puppies may struggle with the hurly burly of the show ring.

You will need to have a very good knowledge of Siberian Husky conformation to guess at how a husky puppy will develop. It is a bit of a lottery, so you may need somebody knowledgeable to accompany you and help you choose.

WORKING DOG

A show dog should also be a working dog, and vice versa, so there should not be a distinction between the two. The conformation of the Siberian Husky, if it is good, will enable him to perform his job well in harness pulling a rig or a sled. The right working attitude is also prized and necessary for a successful dog. Visits to rallies to talk with winning teams and breeders will give you an idea of which dogs have a good attitude and who has the X-factor.

Dogs bred from parents who excel in harness will mean you are more likely to end up with a puppy who will enjoy pulling a rig or sled; he will, hopefully, be a hard worker and will be able to cope with the demands put on a working Siberian. Different dogs play different roles within a large husky team. For example, a good lead dog will be confident to lead a team, but will also be capable of taking and obeying instructions from the dog driver. This is less important for swing/point dogs

HIP SCORING

Whether or not you intend to work your Siberian, it is vitally important that he is healthy and free from pain, and only buying from health tested parents gives you the best chance of ensuring this.

The Siberian usually has very good hips. This is partly due to the need for fitness and working ability that has gone along with the breed over the years, and partly due to the fact that many breed clubs have requirements for health testing, therefore all responsible breeders test every one of their dogs before they are mated. Dogs that appear totally normal can produce puppies with Hip Dysplasia. Environmental factors can worsen the progression of the disease but cannot cause it.

In the UK, the hips can be X-rayed by a vet from the age of 12 months, and the plates are sent away to the British Veterinary Association to be examined by a panel of experts. The scale of points runs from 0 to 53 for each hip. The lower the score, the better the joint.

The Scheme has an average (or mean) score for each breed it covers. The average hip score for the Siberian Husky is 7 – which is the total for BOTH hips.

In the US, the hip scheme is run by the Orthopedic Foundation for Animals (OFA). Dogs must be 24 months old to be tested.

Under the OFA scheme, dogs are rated either "Normal", "Borderline" or "Dysplastic". Only those rated "Normal" will receive a certificate and registration with categories of "Excellent", "Good" or "Fair".

immediately behind the leaders, the team dogs in the body of the team, or the wheel dogs at the back, just ahead of the rig, where a different sort of confidence may be required to handle being in close proximity to a fast-moving vehicle. However, it is useful for your dog to be an all-rounder and be capable of working in all team positions if necessary.

Some dogs, even from good stock, do not enjoy working in a team. This could be to do with personality, or simply because they have had an early bad experience that has knocked their confidence. It is up to you to see that the latter does not happen,

and if you discover that your husky does not have the drive to do what you would like him to do, you must accept the fact and provide other outlets that he might prefer.

TAKING ON AN OLDER DOG

If you feel that a Siberian puppy may not be for you, there is the option of taking on an older dog. Some breeders may keep puppies to see how they develop for either showing or working. Occasionally, these become available if they fail to live up to their early promise, and you may be offered a dog of around eight months to a year.

This can be rewarding, but taking on an adolescent dog and placing him in new circumstances can be stressful for the dog and challenging for you, so make sure you know what you are taking on. For example, if a dog has been brought up with lots of other huskies in an outside run, how will he cope being the only dog living inside in your home? Whilst many huskies are very easy to toilet train, there may well be issues to consider regarding your older dog's early life.

A RESCUED DOG

Unfortunately, more and more Siberians are entering rescue and require homes. Siberians come into rescue for many reasons: marriage break-ups, financial problems, and sometimes because the Siberian himself has not had enough early training and has become unmanageable or too much to handle for that person or family. If you are willing to put in the time and effort needed to help a rescued dog to settle into a new home, rehoming a Siberian can be a brilliant choice and your new companion will often turn out to be an absolute delight and revelation.

Although you will need to do the work, an older dog is often a lot less trouble than a puppy and can be just as rewarding. This is certainly a consideration if you want to get started quickly with any of the husky sports mentioned above. But again, your rescued husky may be an unknown quantity and you will need to go slowly and carefully before doing too much too soon. It may take several weeks for a rescued husky to feel confident and to reveal his true personality to you, but that is part of the charm of taking on a rescue husky.

Huskies are often abandoned simply for displaying the breed traits buyers should have been prepared for.

THE NEW ARRIVAL

The best start you can give your Siberian Husky is to be organised well in advance of his arrival by preparing your house and garden. Huskies do have a reputation for being more destructive than other breeds, although this usually happens if a husky is bored and under stimulated.

The Siberian Husky has been specifically bred to be a working, high-energy, intelligent breed that must be given adequate exercise and mental stimulation on a daily basis. If his needs are catered for, a husky will like nothing better than curling up with you during quiet times; the Siberian adores and needs human companionship. But once he gets an inkling of a walk or a run, he will never refuse, whatever the weather!

IN THE HOME

Firstly, let us look at puppy-proofing your house. The best way to do this is to look at your home from a puppy's perspective. Do those ornaments on the bottom shelf of the cabinet look like play toys? What about the wires from the back of the television, stereo and computer? All of these need to be tucked away and out of harm's way so your pup doesn't amuse himself with a chewing frenzy, which could have disastrous consequences. An important point to remember is that your puppy is not going to be able to distinguish between his 'own' new toys and the much-loved and cherished family teddy bear so, in all cases, keep such items well out of the way. Crawling around on your hands and knees, as well as providing amusement for the rest of the family and friends, will help

to alert you to any potential hazards, as it will allow you to view your home from a four-pawed point of view.

IN THE GARDEN

Next turn your attention to the garden. By now, you will have realised that the Siberian Husky is the Houdini of the dog world, so you must have an adequately fenced garden. This, ideally, means a six-foot (two-metre) fence all round, which cannot be dug under or squeezed through. Do not forget the garden gate; there is no point having a great fence all round if you then have a three-foot (one-metre) gate that can easily be scaled.

Never leave your puppy unsupervised in the garden. There are countless hazards, including finding gaps you never thought existed in the fence, eating snails and slugs, which can cause lungworm and, of course, the one thing no one ever wants to contemplate – dog theft. Pedigree puppies, and particularly the exotic-looking Siberian, can easily be sold on.

BUYING EQUIPMENT

Next you are going to have to embark on a shopping trip to get all the basics you require for your new puppy.

INDOOR CRATE

A crate is invaluable when your Siberian Husky is growing up – and many still choose to use them when they are fully grown. You will need to buy a crate that is big enough to accommodate an adult husky – he must have room to stand up and to turn round. The recommended size is

Most Siberians will be kept in by a six foot fence…

large and ideally, if you have the room, extra large. Your puppy will also need access to water while he is in his crate. This is best provided by buying a bowl that you can attach to the side of the crate.

You will need to decide where you are going to locate the crate. Ideally, this will be in a quiet and draught-free area, such as the kitchen or the utility room, where your dog can sleep and rest undisturbed by the household.

If used correctly, a crate can provide a safe haven for your puppy when he is tired, and at times when you cannot supervise

him. A crate can be useful when initially housetraining your husky, but it does need to be used carefully; a puppy must never be placed in a crate as a punishment.

It is important to take time to introduce your puppy to his crate so that he builds up a good association with it. This can be done by feeding your puppy in the crate and by tossing treats in there. Do not shut him in until he is happy to go in of his own accord, and is happy to settle down and sleep in there.

BEDDING

A lot of breeders will encourage you to take along a piece of clothing or blanket when you visit the puppies. This becomes imbued with the scent of the litter so, when you take your pup home, he has something that smells familiar. You can use this alongside the bedding you are going to provide for your new pup.

If you are using a crate, it will need to be lined with cosy bedding. The best type to buy is the type made of synthetic fleece, which is machine-washable and quick to dry. Buy at least two pieces, so they can be alternated for washing purposes.

BED

Huskies, like all breeds, need a bed they can call home. Some huskies adopt their crate as a permanent base, but many

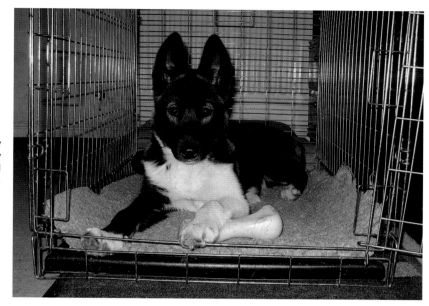

Introduce your puppy gradually to a crate by feeding him in there, and throwing treats in for him.

appreciate a dog bed, which can be located in the main living room.

There is a vast range available from pet stores: for example, there are soft duvet types, both flat and shaped, and hard, plastic ovals, which need to be lined with a soft bed or fleece. Remember: your puppy may well chew his first bed, so wait until he is full grown before you splash out.

BOWLS

You will need two bowls: one for water, which must be freely available and frequently refreshed, and a second for food.

COLLAR AND LEAD

Start by purchasing a small, nylon collar with a simple buckle; this is available as a puppy collar and lead set in most pet shops. As your puppy grows, you will obviously need to let the collar out. In fact, he will quickly grow out of the first collar, so it is not worth buying anything too expensive. The general rule is to allow a two-finger width between your puppy and the collar.

ID

In the UK, by law, a collar should carry some form of identification on it when the dog is in public places. Legal requirements vary according to jurisdiction in the US and Australia, so please check with the relevant body.

The information carried by your dog should include the owner's name and contact details. A lot of husky owners have collars with their details embroidered on, rather than identity discs, which are easily lost.

It is also advisable to use a permanent form of ID, such as microchipping. Microchipping is offered by nearly all veterinary practises and it is usually carried out when your puppy comes in for his second set of vaccinations.

FOOD

When you collect your puppy, most breeders will give you a small amount of food that the puppies have been fed on. If you want to change brands or diet, do so gradually, over the course of a few weeks, so as not to upset your puppy's digestion and cause any further stress to your new arrival.

GROOMING GEAR

You are also going to need grooming brushes for your puppy. It is essential that you acclimatise him to brushing from an early age. Your Sibe is going to shed his coat twice a year – and, boy, are you going to know it! It is essential that you teach your puppy that being brushed is a pleasant event, so always use a brush with soft bristles to start with.

TOYS

Now for the best bit: toys! It is so important to teach your husky puppy to play with toys. Huskies love to chase small furry animals, so we need to give them a natural outlet for this behaviour, which we control in a fun way. You also need to teach your husky that you are the most important being in the world, rather than another dog, a squirrel or a rabbit. You can do this by playing lots of games with your puppy, making them really fun and exciting.

Some of the best toys for husky puppies are large, soft toys, with squeakers in them, which you can move around the floor - your puppy will find this irresistible! Make sure the toys you use are well made and can withstand rough tugging and sharp puppy teeth. Most Sibes also enjoy a tuggy game – knotted tug ropes and fleeces are ideal for this. Make sure you do not tug too hard when your puppy still has his baby teeth and when he is teething, as his gums will be sore at this time. Most importantly, make sure you allow your puppy to win a few games; if you win every time, what is the point in playing? However, make sure you win the final game and put the toy away ready for next time. Your puppy will then learn that you are the source of all the fun things and he should come to you for playtime.

FINDING A VET

The vet will be an important person in your Siberian Husky's life, so it is vital that you find a suitable practice where the vets are accessible and the staff are helpful. It is also important to find out if the vets have had experience of treating husky breeds.

If this is your first dog, ask dog-owning friends and family to find who they recommend and why. Go ahead of time to register and make sure you are happy with the reception you are given. You will also need to find out about emergency cover as well as what facilities are available at the surgery.

Make sure you buy stuffed toys that have been specially made for pets. Toys for children contain flame-retardant stuffing, which can be fatal for dogs if it is consumed.

COLLECTING YOUR PUPPY

At last the day has arrived when you can go to collect your new husky puppy. Ideally, there should be two people to do this – one to drive and one to look after the puppy. Try to collect your puppy as early in the day as possible, so he has time to explore his new home and get settled in before bedtime.

There will be some paperwork to sort out with the breeder, which will include:

- A bill of sale
- A four-generation pedigree
- A contract, which will include an agreement that your puppy cannot be sold on or rehomed without the prior consent of the breeders
- Kennel Club registration papers to transfer ownership of the puppy from the breeder to you
- A diet sheet: This should give advice from puppyhood through to adulthood
- Information on worming and flea treatment
- Vaccination certificate if the puppy has started his inoculations
- Insurance: a Kennel Club registered puppy will generally come with a few weeks' free insurance.

Many breeders will also provide a sample of food to cover the first few days so the puppy does not have to adjust to a new diet.

Ideally, the puppy should be held on your lap for the journey home, so place a blanket on your knees to make it as comfortable as possible. If you have a long car journey, you may need to stop and give your puppy a drink. Do not let him out on the ground if he has not completed his vaccinations.

ARRIVING HOME

As soon as you arrive home, carry your puppy into the garden so he can explore and relieve himself. As soon as he toilets, praise him lavishly and give him a tasty treat – house training has begun! You can then introduce your puppy

Check toys regularly for signs of wear and tear.

Arriving in a new home is a daunting experience – even for the most confident of puppies.

into his new home. Make sure you have already decided on where your puppy is going to eat and sleep, and ensure there is a water bowl already down. Place any blanket or piece of bedding you brought with you from the breeder on to your puppy's bed, so he feels safe and settled. Let your puppy explore his new surroundings; you will probably find that he will wander round for a while and then go to sleep – it will have been a very stressful day for him.

MEETING THE FAMILY
Care must be taken when introducing your puppy to the family. Although it is important that your puppy meets as many new people as possible, you do not want him to be overwhelmed or worried about lots of hands coming towards him. Keep introductions short and fun, rewarding both children and puppy for calm greetings. Try to discourage children from picking your new puppy up, as accidents can easily happen, such as tripping and falling on your pup and also dropping and injuring him.

THE RESIDENT DOG
An older or resident dog may have his nose put out of joint by a new arrival, especially if it is of the younger, playful and sharp-toothed variety. It is important not to disrupt the older dog's existing routine too much, and to make sure he has the opportunity to get away from the pup when he has had enough. Pay him lots of attention – it is all too easy to

forget about him in all the excitement of getting a new puppy.

If at all possible, try to introduce the two dogs on neutral ground, outside the house. Keep a look out for any signs of stress or worry from either of the dogs and intervene if necessary. When overwhelmed, a puppy will roll over and show his tummy to appease the other dog. If he urinates submissively, it is a sign that he is worried, so make sure you look closely for these signs and separate the dogs after a quick hello. All interactions should be supervised for the first few weeks until the pair have sorted out their relationship. If you have to leave them, it is best to make sure your puppy is confined safely in a crate.

Siberians are generally tolerant of a new puppy, but they should be supervised until the pup is well grown and has learned the rules of the pack.

OTHER ANIMALS
Hopefully, you will have done your homework and found out that Siberian Huskies have an incredibly high prey drive. Great care must be taken when introducing smaller or vulnerable animals to your puppy. It may be your child's much-loved pet gerbil – but to your Sibe it is an appetizer.

Cats, rabbits, hamsters, birds all appear on the husky menu, so please do not be lulled into a false sense of security, thinking your puppy will be different.

MEALTIMES
To begin with, feed the diet the puppy is used to, as a change of diet is likely to cause gastric upset. If you want to change the diet, you must do so gradually by adding a tablespoon-size serving of the new food to the existing diet over a period of a few days. This can then be increased to two tablespoon-size servings every few days until your puppy is on the new diet. If your pup suffers from an upset stomach, cut down on the new food and extend the amount of time you take to make the transition.

THE FIRST NIGHT
The first night in a new home is a daunting experience for a puppy, so try to make it as stress-free as possible. He is going to be bewildered and possibly a little afraid. After all, he has been separated from his mother and his littermates for the first time, as well as adjusting to a completely new environment.

How you cope with the first night is open to debate. Some people recommend putting the pup in his crate, where he is safe, and then leaving him to it, ignoring his howls of protest. However, this is a lot to ask of a young puppy, especially as you are leaving him somewhere unfamiliar, where he may hear strange whirring and clicking noises coming from the dishwasher for example, or the central heating.

It is a lot kinder to sleep downstairs with your pup or to have him upstairs by the bed with you. This is when a crate can be really useful. You can put your puppy in the crate, either by the sofa or by the bed, and you can then hang your hand down by the side of the crate so your puppy can be comforted by your physical presence. Ignore any whimpering or crying from your puppy, unless it is very insistent, which may mean your puppy needs to go out to relieve himself.

Take your puppy out at regular intervals and he will soon learn to be clean in the house.

Sleeping close to your pup for the first few nights is also an excellent way of establishing house training as, when he wakes you up, you can take him outside to relieve himself rather than him being left with no option other than to soil his crate or the kitchen floor. You will find that your puppy will settle so much quicker knowing that someone is there and it will increase your bond with your husky immensely.

Over the space of a week or two, you can gradually move the crate further away from the bed or sofa, as your husky will now be feeling so much safer and more secure in his surroundings and will have grown in confidence. Finally, you can move your puppy to where you would like him to sleep permanently.

HOUSE TRAINING
Siberian Huskies are a clean and intelligent breed and, as such, they are usually very easy to house train. The key to house training is to reward your puppy when he goes to the toilet where you want him to – it really is as simple as that.

You will need to anticipate when your puppy will need to relieve himself. This will be:
• First thing in the morning
• After mealtimes
• Immediately after a play session
• When he wakes from a nap
• Last thing at night.

In addition, you will need to take your puppy out into the garden at regular intervals – which means every hour – so he is given the opportunity to toilet.

Always accompany your puppy

into the garden and stay with him while he performs. It can be slightly disheartening, standing in gale force wind and horizontal rain while your puppy mooches about deciding whether he wants to squat, but this is essential training and the short-term discomfort pays back ten-fold in the long term. As soon as your puppy has relieved himself, offer him a tasty treat and praise him lavishly. Make sure you do this every time your puppy performs; consistency is very important.

WHEN ACCIDENTS HAPPEN

There are always going to be times when your puppy starts to squat in the house. If this happens, clap your hands or make a startling noise, and immediately usher your pup outside. As soon as he performs, reward and praise him.

If your puppy has an accident in the house, do not punish him in any way. Simply put him out of the way while you clear up the mess. Your pup will learn very quickly that he would much rather have lavish praise and a treat for toileting in the garden, rather than being ignored in the house. Huskies are very eager to please and love praise and attention. If

A baby gate, or specially made dog gate, is ideal for keeping your dog out of harm's way, and will also accustom a puppy to spending time on his own.

you are consistent with this approach, it will only take a few days for your puppy to understand what you are asking him to do. It is worth remembering, though, that all puppies will occasionally 'forget' themselves and that odd accidents are all part and parcel of having a puppy in the house.

HOUSE RULES

As a family, it is a good idea to decide on some ground rules, such as whether your husky is going to be allowed on the sofa. It is unfair and confusing to a puppy to find when he has grown a bit that he is no longer welcome on the couch at night. Consistency is the key to having a happy, relaxed and well-behaved pet.

You will probably decide to give your husky boundaries within the house, especially when he is young and still being house trained. The easiest way to do this is to use child gates; the kitchen is the best place to contain a puppy, as the flooring is usually the most suitable to cope with any toilet training accidents, but child gates can also be used to stop a puppy from going upstairs unsupervised. Containing your puppy in one room like this is also a good substitute for using a crate.

A child gate can also be a useful training tool, teaching your puppy to spend time alone. Huskies are very social dogs and they love and need to spend lots of time with their human 'pack', but we need to teach a puppy how to be relaxed when he is away from us so he does not develop behaviour problems later on in life.

HANDLING AND GROOMING

Getting your husky pup used to being handled is important, not only for the annual trip to your vet for a check-up but also in case of an accident, such as a cut pad while out walking.

You should start getting your puppy used to being handled as soon as he is settled into his new home. You can start by gently feeling your pup all over, along his back, underneath and all the way down his tail. You can gently feel between the pads, check his ears and eyes, and part his lips to examine his gums and teeth. You must make this all very rewarding for your puppy; a good way to do this is to feed little treats while you are feeling him all over.

If your puppy is unsure about being handled, such as when you lift his paws or open his mouth, just slow down all your movements and practise little and often, using treats as a reward for calm behaviour.

Grooming is also going to be an important part of your lives together, and, boy, can huskies moult! There is a joke among Sibe owners that huskies only moult once a year – but it lasts 12 months! It is really important that your puppy learns to love being brushed. To start with, you just need a soft brush so your puppy gets used to the sensation

Ideally, a Siberian should travel in a crate where he is safe and secure.

of being groomed. As always reward your puppy with tasty treats throughout and only brush your puppy for a couple of minutes at a time.

WEARING A COLLAR

If your puppy has not worn a collar before, he may spend a lot of time scratching at it, just because it is something very new and alien to him. To get him used to wearing the collar, practise putting it on for a few minutes at a time while playing with your pup so he is distracted by something that is fun. Similarly, you could put the collar on your pup when you are feeding him, so he associates something nice with the new sensation.

For safety's sake, it is always best to remove your puppy's collar if you are leaving him alone for any period of time, just in case it gets snagged on something and your pup cannot free himself. Always remove your puppy's collar at night; this is more comfortable for him and it serves as a signal that now is the time to settle down.

OUT AND ABOUT

Socialising your puppy can never start too soon. In order to have a happy, relaxed and well-behaved husky, you need to get him out and about, meeting as many people and dogs as possible and experiencing all sorts of sights and sounds.

For more information, see Chapter Six: Training and Socialisation.

CAR TRAVEL

Travelling with your husky in a car is going to take some consideration. Whatever his age, your husky should be secured in a vehicle at all times – he should never be allowed to be loose in the car. This is for both your sakes; if you have to brake suddenly and your dog is loose on the back seat, he will be flung forward, either towards the back of your neck or the windscreen. I am sure you can work out the horrific consequences of that.

Remember, if you only ever take your husky to the vet in your car he will soon learn to dread going in it, so lots of short fun trips as a puppy are ideal. Even if you just drive a mile or so to your local park, your husky will soon be breaking the door down to accompany you.

Never leave your husky in a car on a warm day. Cars, even in the shade and with the windows dropped, can be a deadly place to leave a dog as temperatures rise very rapidly.

AN OLDER DOG

Much of the advice on settling in a puppy can be applied to taking on an older or rescued dog, especially if you have little background history and are unsure as to whether he is house trained or not. An older dog may have been used to a slightly different routine and handling, so it is important that kind and consistent methods are shown to ensure that your new husky settles happily into the family home. Younger children should be supervised around rescued dogs, as you will not be sure of previous experiences.

If you have existing dogs in the household and are introducing a new canine member, try to ensure you spend twice as much time with your new dog as the resident dog(s) do. This ensures that your new Sibe creates a bond with you rather than the other dogs.

SUMMING UP

There is an old saying that goes along the lines of: 'You only get out, what you put in', and this adage is perfect when you apply

it to bringing up a Siberian puppy. The more time, work and effort you put into training and socialising your new family member, the more rounded, well behaved and fun your dog will be

later in life. By adopting kind and consistent training methods, your puppy will be a willing and intelligent student who will be a pleasure to own and will be welcome wherever you go.

An older dog needs kindness and consideration to help him settle in a new home.

THE BEST OF CARE

5 Chapter

When you purchase your Siberian Husky, it is hard to think beyond the first few weeks, focusing on the fun and challenges of getting your new best friend through puppyhood. However, dog ownership is a lifetime commitment and it is important to address the issues around your dog's life. Sometimes the novelty of owning a dog can wane and, all too often, a dog can become a nuisance and hindrance to all the other things you want to do.

Huskies love to be part of the family, so you need to ensure that your dog is well trained from a young age so that he is well adjusted and is able to accompany you wherever you go. A varied and interesting schedule will ensure a good quality of life for as long as your husky lives. After you have completed puppy training, try some follow-on training to really bed in your Sibe's education – and there is a whole range of dog sports to get involved in. The beauty of further training classes is that your dog will learn to continue to respond to you and keep a close connection rather than going off and getting up to mischief. Into the bargain, you will meet lots of sympathetic doggie people and learn more about dogs in general as well as finding out more about your dog and what he is really capable of.

For more information on training and dog sports, see Chapter Six: Training and Socialisation.

DIET AND NUTRITION
The dog food business is a multimillion-pound industry and everyone you speak to will have opinions about what they consider the most suitable diet. There are a number of feeding methods and it is important that you choose not only a food that suits your dog, but that also suits you and your family. There is little point deciding on a home-cooked diet when you barely have time or opportunity to cook for yourself. You also need to bear in mind the origins of the Siberian Husky – what they were bred for, and the extreme conditions they worked in – when deciding on the most suitable diet.

COMPLETE FOODS
With complete food, you do get what you pay for and the cheaper brands tend to use additives and a high sugar content to make them more palatable. There are a number of holistic brands of complete food on the market,

SPECIALISED DIGESTION

One of the commonest problems that new husky owners ask about is diarrhoea. This can happen because of stress, a change of water or an infection, but the most usual cause is overfeeding, or feeding the wrong sort of food.

The Siberian Husky's digestive systems has adapted to cope with the food that is commonly found in the harsh environment of the far north, where there is very little vegetation and almost no cereal. Because of this, they do best when fed on a quality diet, high in fat and protein with a very low cereal content. Your puppy's breeder will have raised the litter on a suitable food and can advise you on what is best.

If a puppy eats too much cereal-based food, he or she is likely to have a serious digestive upset and this will cause diarrhoea. It is important to bear in mind that a lot of Siberians are sensitive to rice. Therefore, the common advice to feed plain chicken and rice to a dog that has an upset stomach will often make a husky worse.

The other common reason for a Siberian to have diarrhoea is overfeeding. Again, this is a result of their Arctic origins. Food was not always easily available and so sled dogs were bred to be able to work well on very small amounts of high-fat food. They do not need the quantity of food that other breeds do, and if they are fed too much, they will not be able to digest it and will get diarrhoea. Reducing the quantity fed at each meal and giving an extra small meal to make up for it will often help solve the problem.

Diarrhoea is one of the conditions that can seem minor, but in puppies it can be life-threatening if not treated quickly. A young puppy can dehydrate alarmingly quickly, and if your pup is vomiting as well, this is a very serious situation. Consult your vet as soon as possible.

which contain only natural ingredients. Although these do tend to be more expensive, you feed a smaller amount, as they have better nutritional content than their cheaper counterparts. Complete food is just that, so there is no need to add any supplements or other food to it. Indeed, doing so can cause health problems, as you will be nutritionally unbalancing the feed.

Remember to ensure that fresh drinking water is available at all times. This is especially important if you decide to feed a complete food, as it can make your dog thirsty. Some people moisten the food with either tepid or cold water to enhance the smell and encourage the dog to eat.

There are different preparations of food aimed at all the stages of life that your husky will go through – puppy, junior, adult, senior, etc. If you decide to feed a complete food, it is important to work out the correct amount of food to feed your dog from the guidelines supplied by the manufacturer, and make sure you guard against over feeding.

There is no need to add supplements to a complete diet.

Most dogs find canned food very appetising.

You need a reliable supplier if you decide to feed fresh meat.

THE BARF DIET

This diet is based on the principle of feeding as near to a natural diet as possible. Bones and Raw Food or Biologically Appropriate Raw Food (BARF) includes raw meats but no grain-based carbohydrates. It is said by the originator of the diet, Dr Ian Billinghurst, that dogs cannot digest carbohydrate, which can result in many health problems.

Many people are feeding this diet with good results, but you will need to do your own research and seek advice from people in the breed before you give it a try.

COOKED MEAT AND BISCUIT

There is a very wide variety of canned and sachets of meat available, again ranging from cheap to expensive. Most of these provide a complete balanced diet, although some of the brands benefit from the addition of a biscuit mixer. There

are some complete 'wet' dog foods that are also holistic and contain no preservatives or additives. These do tend be very palatable to dogs, although they can work out expensive to feed all the time. Again, this method of feeding can be convenient for travelling with your dog, as long as you don't have half packets to store in between meals.

FEEDING PUPPIES

It is best to be guided by your breeder, but most puppies will be on four meals a day when they first come to you and these should be spread out evenly throughout the day. This is gradually reduced down to three and then, at around six months, to two.

The key to feeding your puppy is little and often, but this must be carefully timed around toileting and exercise. It is usually best to feed your pup half an hour after he has been

outside for his morning constitutional and bolt round the garden. Never feed your puppy (or adult dog) before exercise: not only is it uncomfortable for the dog, but it can cause gastric torsion, a life-threatening condition, where the stomach fills with gas and twists.

FEEDING ADULTS

It is best to have a feeding routine, preferably feeding two smaller meals a day when your dog is fully grown. Occasionally, you can come across a puppy or dog who is a fussy eater. Do not fall into the trap of constantly swapping foods to find a brand that your dog likes or by adding tasty treats to the food to make it more 'interesting'. By doing this your dog will start to hold out for more and more tasty treats, as he will learn that by not eating his food straight away he will be rewarded later on.

At mealtimes, put your dog's

PROVIDING BONES

All dogs, regardless of their age, need opportunities to gnaw and chew. There are some small risks associated with feeding bones, such as splintering or injuring teeth, but these seem to be rare.

Never leave your dog with a bone; he should always be supervised. Never feed cooked bones to your dog, as they are dangerous. They can easily splinter and lodge in the intestine, or cause choking – both of which could be fatal.

Your Siberian will enjoy gnawing on a real bone, but make sure he is supervised. Although medium-sized dogs, Siberians can demolish smaller chew toys in no time. The larger Nylabones, however, are ideal.

food down for approximately 15 minutes; whatever is left after that period of time, lift up and put to one side. Fussy eaters soon learn the routine after a couple days and will eagerly eat if they are hungry. Feeding in this way means you know when it is safe to exercise your dog, as you know when he last ate and also when to do a training session – there is little point trying to motivate a satiated husky! Do not, therefore, be tempted to leave food down for your puppy to graze on throughout the day.

DANGERS OF OBESITY

Never allow your Husky to get overweight: the extra body weight puts pressure on the joints and vital organs and can cause long-term health problems. The best way to ensure your dog is a healthy weight is to check that he has a 'waist'. Looking down on your dog, he should 'go in' slightly where the ribs finish. If you have an extra furry husky, try feeling for the ribs, which should be easily discernible with a layer of fat covering them. If in doubt, consult your veterinary nurse for advice or a reputable husky breeder whom you know and trust. If you have had your husky spayed or neutered, it may be necessary to reduce his or her food a little, as the reduction in hormones can affect the metabolic rate, meaning fewer calories are required.

When calculating the quantity to feed, remember to count in the treats you feed in the overall diet as well.

Never allow your Siberian to become overweight, as this can lead to health problems. Ribs should be easy to find under a thin layer of fat.

GROOMING A HUSKY

Grooming is obviously an important cosmetic aspect for showing, but it has many health benefits, which include stimulating circulation and removing foreign bodies that may cause skin irritation. By grooming your husky regularly you get to know his contours and body temperature intimately so that you can easily tell when something is not quite right.

It is therefore important to get your husky used to being groomed and handled on a daily basis. Many huskies are quite resistant to 'beauty measures' so you will need to take it slowly. There will be certain areas of the body that your husky will take exception to. Most huskies will hate having their tail messed with. As the tail is an extension of your dog's spine, handling must be gentle and careful. Paws and

mouth areas can also be sites of dispute, but it is, of course, important that you can gain easy access in cases of injury or emergency. For example, your husky may cut his pad or he may get something stuck in his throat.

A lot of huskies do not like being grabbed by the neck. You may find that your husky dislikes his collar being pulled over his head and will show his dislike by mouthing at your hands.

Siberians, like most sled dogs, moult a lot and during this time they look positively motheaten!

A rake designed for double-coated dogs is the best tool to use when the coat is shedding.

To prevent this happening right from the start, it is vital to handle all areas when you do not need to. Wait until your husky is well rested and relaxed and spend time gently putting your puppy's collar on and off very loosely, and rewarding calm behaviour with praise and treats. The same goes with his tail, feet and any other areas your dog does not like being handled. Start with the least worrying part of his body and gradually work to the areas of contention. Only reach slowly, and very briefly, for your puppy's paw, for example, after having got him used to having his leg stroked. Reward him, leave it for a while, and then repeat. Do not grab or squeeze sensitive areas until your dog is regularly at ease with the procedure.

GROOMING ROUTINE

Grooming is an aspect of husky care that can be neglected because many huskies have shortish coats, and the need for a grooming regime is not at first apparent when your husky is a puppy. Indeed, if you leave a mucky puppy without attention, you will find that in half and hour he will have cleaned himself up as if by magic. However, it is not always a good idea to leave a dog to dry off naturally, especially if he is very young or getting on in years.

Regardless of whether your husky gets mucky or not, come the first moult you will soon realise that grooming is going to be a major part of your husky's life if you are not going to suffocate under a blanket of dog hair floating through your home environment!

Your grooming kit need not be extensive, but it should include a variety of brushes, a couple of doggie towels and nail clippers.

TOWEL DRY

Firstly, get your dog used to being towel-dried. Failure to do this may mean that your husky will dash into your house and leap on to the sofa to dry himself off on your upholstery. The Siberian seems to have a particular penchant for rubbing his face over your favourite cushions!

Super-absorbent towels for

humans are good for soaking up an excess of wet lying on the surface of your husky's thick double coat. Tummy, chest, legs and groin that are less well covered with hair get very wet and should be dried off to prevent chafing and for the protection of your carpets and cushions.

BRUSHING

Your dog may need a rake or curry comb-type brush depending where he is in the moulting cycle. An ordinary brush is OK for the finishing touches but will not remove the mountain of hair that appears on your dog but does not drop without encouragement. A rake is good for the back leg feathers and for the top guard hairs but often a curry comb with a mat of spines can get to grips with a dropping undercoat. Beware, though. You can have a good grooming session one day only to wake up the following morning to find your dog looking once more like a yeti with tufts of hair poking out all over the place.

COMBING

A comb can also do a good job, although dogs are less keen on the pulling sensation it causes, so you will need to go gently. However, a comb is good for removing the hair that is clogging up your brushes. To emphasise just how much hair can be shed by huskies, some owners have used their dog hair to make woollen jumpers, hats and scarves!

NAIL CLIPPING

If you exercise your husky on hard ground then nails should wear down without the need for nail clipping. However, huskies have side dewclaws that do not wear down and these will need to be trimmed from time to time. Be careful not to cut through the pink vein or 'quick' that runs down the inside of the nail. Many veterinary practices will offer a nail clipping service for a small fee, but you should still get your dog used to having his paws handled and to having his nails trimmed to prevent this becoming a stressful event for your dog and veterinary nurse.

DENTAL CARE

Teething can be a stressful time for both puppy and owner, but it is normal and often a lot of the puppy's milk teeth will disappear without you noticing. Siberian puppies love chewing anyway, but when the adult teeth start to appear, it is very important to provide your pup with safe toys to chew on. You can ease sore gums by giving him ice cubes; thick rope chews are also ideal.

Very occasionally you will find that the canine teeth or fangs do not fall out as soon as the adult teeth come through, and a puppy will have both for a short time. This is only a concern if the milk tooth presses against the adult tooth and causes it to become misplaced. Your vet will be able to advise you on whether a retained milk tooth needs to be removed, and this is a fairly straightforward procedure.

While your puppy is teething, be careful not to handle his mouth in a way that is uncomfortable, as

Accustom your Siberian to nail trimming from an early age.

Brush your dog's teeth with a soft toothbrush and special dog toothpaste (as human toothpaste can be very harmful to dogs).

this can make the dog shy of people's hands and could even lead to him becoming nervous of being handled

Finger brushes are a good way to start your husky getting used to the sensation of having his teeth cleaned. Start by gently massaging the gums with this and gradually you can progress to a soft doggie toothbrush and a recommended doggie toothpaste. In addition, dog chews and bones will help to eliminate tartar and retain your dog's 'film star smile'!

It is important not to exercise your dog, or let him run around like mad, for a couple of hours after feeding. He needs time to digest his food properly. At worst this can lead to bloat (see page 139), especially in older dogs.

MASSAGE

Canine massage is also another way of forming a connection with your dog and can be adapted for all aspects of your dog's life: puppy massage, canine sports massage, and therapeutic massage for the older or arthritic dog. Most dogs enjoy being massaged and it can be very helpful in preparing for exercise or for supporting the older dog. There are several books on the subject available or you could embark on a dog massage course. Your dog will certainly enjoy the attention!

EXERCISE

This is going to a huge part of both your lives! Regardless of the weather (unless it is really hot)

you are going to be out and about an awful lot, so if you didn't know the local countryside, go and buy maps and a decent pair of walking shoes.

As with all breeds, young Husky puppies should not be over-exercised – this means not allowing them to walk too far, which could damage their young, vulnerable joints. It is a fine line with such an active breed to get a balance of physical and mental stimulation right. Lots of short walks are preferable to one or two longer outings – this gives your husky a chance to sleep and recharge his batteries in between adventures.

As the husky is such an intelligent breed, it is worth

remembering that physical exercise alone will not tire out your puppy. He needs play and training sessions to engage his brain, which will, in turn, make him weary. The same applies to an adult husky; this is a breed that needs extensive physical exercise, but this must be combined with mental stimulation.

THE OLDER HUSKY

Huskies can live for 15 years or more, although the average for the breed is considerably lower than this. However, with luck, you will share many years together and enjoy some unique and truly unforgettable moments. One thing is certain: once you open your door and your heart to a

Siberians are a working breed and even those kept as pets or show dogs must have an outlet for their abundant energy and stamina.

husky, your life will never quite be the same again.

Huskies tend to stay fairly active for most of their lives and show little signs of slowing down in comparison to some other breeds. A lot of huskies will still enjoy racing in harness until double figures and canicross dogs will certainly get the hump and sulk if you hang up their running shoes too soon. It is, of course, necessary to recognise the signs that your dog is becoming more senior and will no longer want to go out for as far or as fast as he once did. However, this is no excuse to put away your walking shoes; senior dogs still require regular exercise. Shorter, more frequent walks, such as they had

in puppyhood, are ideal and this will also help the ageing bladder.

If you are short of interesting walks from home, pop your dog in the car and drive him to different places so he is kept alert mentally and challenged by new smells, sights and sounds.

As your husky gets older, he may start to get stiff joints. Fortunately, there are plenty of veterinary preparations that can help to alleviate this and, indeed, give your older husky a new lease of life. The stiffness will be most notable when your husky initially gets up, and perhaps after a walk, when he has overdone it a little.

Older dogs will also tend to sleep more, so it is important that your husky's bed is comfortable

and in a draught-free and quiet area of the house. You will sometimes find that an older dog no longer sleeps curled up in a ball as he did when he was younger. This is because it is not as comfortable, as his joints as stiffer, so he prefers to sleep stretched out.If this is the case, a change of bed could make life much more comfortable.

If you have a younger dog or young children at home, make sure that your golden oldie has a safe haven to escape to when he needs some peace and quiet, away from noise and activity. Older dogs can be a little grumpy, especially if they are feeling stiff and sore or disorientated, or if they are woken suddenly and they are struggling to adjust immediately to their surroundings.

As in humans, an older dog may start to lose some of his senses, such as hearing and eyesight, although your dog's sense of smell will remain very keen. If you suspect your dog is losing his sight or hearing, try to compensate by not moving furniture around and using exaggerated hand signals when training.

Some older dogs can also develop urinary incontinence; this is more common if they have been neutered or spayed. If you suspect that your husky is 'leaking', seek help from your vet, as there are medications that can be prescribed.

The most important thing to remember about your ageing husky is to be patient and understanding. Your husky is still the same dog you loved as a puppy and as a fit, athletic adult,

and your feelings towards him should never change. It is now your turn to look after his needs and reward him for all the wonderful devotion he has shown you.

LETTING GO
This sadly leads to the moment you must say goodbye to your best friend. Whether it is through sudden illness or old age, as loving owners we have to make the decision to alleviate our

Older huskies tend to stay quite active but you should be aware of your dog's changing needs.

friend's suffering. Sometimes it is a clear-cut case and your vet will advise you that it is in your pet's best interest to put an end to his or her suffering. Other times it may not be so obvious, but do not let your pet struggle on in pain, and try not to put your own feelings ahead of those of your faithful companion. Your vet will, hopefully, by now be a good friend, who will offer guidance and comfort when you need it.

If you have the luxury of time, you can decide how and where your best friend should slip away. Most vets will happily arrange to visit you at home, so that your dog is not put through a last and stressful visit to the veterinary surgery. As hard as it may be, you owe it your husky to be there at the end, holding him and reassuring him as he slips away. Luckily, he will have little idea of what is happening as he gently falls into his final sleep.

Your husky will have been your companion, friend and a huge part of your life, and he deserves all the comfort and reassurance that you can give him at this final goodbye. Keep reassuring and comforting him and try not to be overcome by your own emotions at the end - hold back until your friend has gone, so he can feel calm and serene while he slips away.

Given time, the pain of losing your best friend diminishes and you can look back on all the amazing experiences and the

When the time comes to say goodbye to your elderly Siberian, try to remember all the good times you spent together.

abundance of laughs you had together, to celebrate a wonderful lifetime and a unique friendship. Eventually, when the time is right,

you might consider welcoming another husky into your life – and this will be the start of a whole new chapter…

SOCIALISATION AND TRAINING

Chapter 6

When you decided to bring a Siberian Husky into your life, you probably had dreams of how it was going to be: long walks together, cosy evenings with a husky lying devotedly at your feet and, whenever you returned home, there would always be a special welcome waiting for you.

There is no doubt that you can achieve all this – and much more – with a Siberian Husky, but like anything that is worth having, you must be prepared to put in the work. A husky, regardless of whether he is a puppy or an adult, does not come ready trained, understanding exactly what you want and fitting perfectly into your lifestyle. It is therefore your mission to teach him, with kindness, consistency and understanding, what is acceptable behaviour.

We have a great starting point in that the breed is intelligent and outgoing – he loves his family and wants to be involved in everything that is going on in his home. However, it is important to remember that the Siberian also has an independent streak: he thinks for himself and will become focused on what interests him most, be it a rabbit, a squirrel or a bird. When you train your husky, you will need to be creative and try to get on his wavelength in order to bring out the best in him.

THE FAMILY PACK

Dogs have been domesticated for some 14,000 years and they have inherited and retained behaviour from their distant ancestor – the wolf. A Siberian Husky may never have lived in the wild, but he is born with the survival skills and the mentality of a meat-eating predator who hunts in a pack. A wolf living in a pack owes its existence to mutual co-operation, as this ensures both food and protection. A domesticated dog living in a family pack has exactly the same outlook – and this applies most particularly to the Siberian Husky, who was bred to live and work in a pack. He wants food and companionship and it is your job to provide for these needs.

YOUR ROLE

As soon as your puppy arrives in your home it is up to you to show your puppy in a fair, compassionate manner how to behave so that he will look to you to make all the important decisions. This does not mean that you have to act like a dictator or a bully.

Have you got what it takes to be a firm, fair and consistent leader?

If you think what makes a good boss, the chances are you will describe someone who provides fair boundaries where the goalposts do not change – even when under stress – and someone who understands and helps you out when you are struggling or not sure what to do. A good boss will show you where you are going wrong without punishing you, will praise you when doing well, and will reward you for a job well done. If you can be this sort of leader to your Siberian, you will not go far wrong.

Conversely, a bad leader and friend will be someone who shouts or hits you when you go wrong, will manhandle you when in a temper to get you to do what they want and will be unpredictable, giving you one direction one day and an opposite command the next day according to their mood. Such a boss will make you anxious and eventually unresponsive because you are worried about doing the wrong thing, but you are not sure what the right thing is!

HOW TO BE A GOOD LEADER

- **Keep it simple:** Decide on the rules you want your husky to obey and always make it 100 per cent clear by showing him what is acceptable behaviour.
- **Be consistent:** If you are not consistent about enforcing rules, how can you expect your husky to understand what is required? There is nothing worse than allowing your dog to jump on the sofa one moment and then scolding him the next time he does it because he is muddy. Your husky will not necessarily realise why he can jump on the sofa in one situation and not in another. Bear in mind, inconsistency leads to insecurity and potential behavioural issues.
- **Get your timing right:** It is important to reward your husky's good behaviour within one or two seconds of the event, otherwise your dog will not link this behaviour with your reaction.
- **Try to ignore or, better still, prevent what you consider to be bad behaviour by putting your dog in a position to do the right thing.** Many huskies get up to all sorts of mischief, so you could spend a lot of time saying "no" or reprimanding your husky and this is dispiriting for you and demotivating for him. He will eventually switch off and ignore you altogether or, in extreme circumstances, question your

authority, which will lead to confrontation and an escalation in the severity of your reprimands, which is highly undesirable. This may also make your training more difficult.

- **Read your dog's body language:** Find out how to read body language and facial expressions (see page 80) so that you understand your husky's feelings and intentions.
- **Be aware of your own body language:** You can also help your dog to learn by using your body language to communicate with him. For example, if you want your dog to come to you, open your arms out and look inviting. Dogs do not come ready trained so you will need to show them first what you mean by commands.
- **Tone of voice:** Dogs do not speak English; they learn by associating a word with the required action. However, they are very receptive to tone of voice, so you can use your voice to praise him. If you are pleased with your Siberian Husky, praise him to the skies in a warm, happy voice so that he knows he has done well.
- **Give one command only:** If you keep repeating a command, or keeping changing it, it will lose its meaning as far as your husky is concerned or he will not understand what you mean. When giving a command try to assess whether your husky is likely to pay attention; if you think he will ignore you, do not give the command. If he does

Teaching your Siberian to "Wait" in a car teaches him to inhibit his natural exuberance – but make sure he cannot dart past you.

not respond the first time you ask, make it simple by using a treat to lure him into position and then you can reward him for a correct response. Repeat as many times as is necessary. Make sure all members of your family use the same words and handsignals to reinforce your training and not confuse your Sibe.

- **Daily reminders:** A young Siberian Husky is apt to forget his manners from time to time and an adolescent dog may appear to have forgotten all his training (he hasn't!). Rather than coming down on him like a ton of bricks when he does something wrong, try to do some training every day so you have the opportunity to remind your dog and reinforce the behaviours you want and

prevent him from getting up to activities that are less desirable. After all, we are all likely to repeat behaviours that we know will be rewarded. Remember to reward often while he is learning; only reduce treats and rewards once he has learned his lessons well. Even then, random bonuses for a job well done throughout his lifetime will keep up the good behaviour.

Try the following:

- Practise asking your husky to wait in the car so that he learns not to leap out of the back of the vehicle, which could be potentially lethal. It is also important for dogs, and especially puppies, not to leap too great distances, as shoulder injuries can easily occur.
- Teach your dog to follow you

through doorways so that he does not barge ahead.

* If you do not want a dog to beg at the table, ensure you do not feed him while you are eating.

• When you are playing with your husky, allow him to win some games – after all, who would play a game they always lose? However, it might be a good idea to win more games than you lose. When your husky comes to you with the toy, do not always take it off him. You have probably worked hard to get him interested in a toy – so keep the fun going. If you want the toy, produce another toy that he likes even better and swap it for the first toy, or use food so that your husky learns that relinquishing his toy brings

even better things. In this way your Sibe will learn to give up the toy when you ask because he associates it with something else nice happening. Physically forcing your dog to give up a toy will not be pleasant. That is a sure way to make him run off with a toy if he thinks he is going to lose it every time he plays with you. Running after your dog for his toy, or even your favourite slipper, may also be viewed as a game - with you in the unenviable position of being led a merry dance by your husky.

UNDERSTANDING YOUR SIBERIAN HUSKY

Body language is an important means of communication

between dogs, which they use to make friends, to assert status and to avoid conflict. It is important to get on your dog's wavelength by understanding his body language and reading his facial expressions. Research has shown that the Siberian Husky has a wider repertoire of communication skills than most other breeds. This ties in with his wolf-like appearance; it is the breeds that look most like their ancestors that have a wider range of expressions.

The most obvious signals to look for are:

• A relaxed body posture and a low, slow-wagging tail indicate a happy, confident dog. A fast-wagging tail can indicate arousal, which may be good or

A dog that raises his hackles may be feeling anxious, annoyed or just over-excited.

THE VOCAL HUSKY

The Siberian Husky has a reputation for being a noisy breed that barks a lot, but this is not the case. A husky will howl and vocalise rather than bark, although he may give an alarm "yip" to warn of someone's arrival. A Siberian will vocalise when he is playing, and some are yodellers, which seems to be a sign of excitement and pleasure.

The Siberian Husky's howl is a breed characteristic and a group howl is truly awesome in its volume, harmony and tunefulness. This can be triggered by different situations, but dogs that live in a pack will set up a group howl if a couple of their number are taken out separately. It generally lasts for about 30 seconds before subsiding – a consideration if you live in a built-up area…

Howling can be triggered by a variety of different situations.

'bad' depending on the reaction of the other dog.
- A crouched body posture with ears back and tail down shows that a dog is being submissive. A dog may do this when he is being told off or if a more assertive dog approaches him.
- A bold dog will stand tall, looking strong and alert. His ears will be forward and his tail will be held high. This is particularly characteristic of a confident husky.
- A dog who raises his hackles (lifting the fur along his topline) is trying to make himself look bigger; he is likely to be anxious or worried, which may have implications for his next behaviour.
- A playful dog will go down on his front legs while standing on his hind legs in a bow position. This friendly invitation says: "I'm no threat, let's play."
- A dog challenging another of his species will meet them with a hard stare. If he is challenged, he may bare his teeth and growl and the corners of his mouth will be drawn forward. His ears will be forward and he will

Most Siberians will see food treats as a reward that is worth working for.

appear tense in every muscle.

- A nervous dog will often show aggressive behaviour as a means of self-protection. If threatened, this dog will lower his head and flatten his ears. The corners of his mouth may be drawn back and he may bark or whine.
- If your husky shows worried, aggressive or nervous behaviour, he will not be feeling at all happy, and it is your job as his best friend to confidently and gently remove him from the negative situation so that he has some space. If your dog is showing these behaviours and you are not sure why, then avoid the situations that caused the behaviour and consult an experienced dog behaviourist to help you help your husky deal with his anxieties. We all know how uncomfortable it is to feel anxious, so see it from your dog's point of view and get him some help.

GIVING REWARDS

By being a kind, fair companion, a husky will learn to rely on you to make the important decisions. This can be difficult for your inquisitive husky, whose thoughts of unquestioning obedience may be challenged by the sight of a rabbit or a really enticing scent. The answer is that you must try to be the most interesting, the most attractive and the most irresistible person in your husky's eyes. It would be nice to think that you could achieve this by personality alone, but most of us need a little extra help. You need to find out what is the biggest reward for your dog. In most cases, a Siberian Husky will be motivated to work for food reward. Some prefer a game, but as this may involve dismembering the toy before proceeding to the next exercise, it is sometimes not the right tool for the job! The golden rule is: whatever reward you use, make sure it is something that your dog really wants.

When you are teaching a dog a new exercise, you should reward your husky frequently. When he knows the exercise or command, reward him randomly so that he keeps on responding to you in a positive manner.

If your husky does something extra special, make sure he really knows how pleased you are by giving him a handful of treats. If he gets a bonanza reward, he is more likely to repeat the behaviour on future occasions.

TOP TREATS
You can grade your rewards according to the difficulty of the exercise. Lower-grade treats can include your dog's normal biscuit ration or food that he is not wildly excited about. Every dog is different and it is up to you to find out what turns your husky on! Higher-grade treats will include cooked liver, sausage and cheese.

Lower-grade treats can be used for exercises where your husky has already achieved some success in a familiar and quiet, undistracting environment.

Higher-grade treats should be used for new exercises with which your Sibe is unfamiliar, for exercises he finds difficult (such as recall in a busy environment) and for exercises he knows but that you are practising in a distracting or unfamiliar environment.

If your dog does not take a treat in certain circumstances, it could be that he is full, ill or worried. You will need to use your dog skills to ascertain which this might be.

Whatever type of treat you use, you should remember to subtract it from your husky's daily food ration. The Siberian Husky has a lean, athletic build, and you want to keep it that way. Dogs that are overweight are lethargic, prone to health problems and will almost certainly have a shorter life expectancy, so reward your husky, but always keep a check on his figure!

TOP TOYS
Dogs are descended from predators and will therefore be programmed to chase things in order to catch prey. Playing with toys gives them an outlet for this impulse, and toy play is a great way to bond with your husky.

Soft toys made of fake fur and fleece will be attractive to the teething puppy with a sensitive mouth. He will enjoy a tuggy game (but remember not to shake your puppy's head around too much!). Unfortunately, your husky is usually also a demolition demon and if left alone may disembowel your brand new fleecy toy/tennis ball/expensive new slippers (he cannot make this distinction) and may be tempted to ingest the fleece, stuffing or even the squeaker.

This can obviously be dangerous, so you will need to supervise your dog around these toys and, better still, only use

A kong will keep your husky occupied when he is spending time on his own. Make sure you buy the heavier duty variety as the Siberian is a stong chewer.

them to play with your dog. Do not leave them lying around the house for your puppy to demolish or get bored with. Gather them up into a dog toy box out of reach and let your dog have a different new toy every day. In this way your puppy is more likely to want to play with the toy you are offering, and it gives him the message that you are the provider of all exciting things.

Interactive toys will be easy for your dog to get hold of. You should try to keep these toys exciting by moving them in an erratic manner and making them unpredictable so you keep your dog focused on them. Sometimes attaching a bit of rope to a toy and dragging it along the ground for your husky to follow will give him loads of fun. Throwing a toy and chasing after it will encourage a bit of competition and add to the fun of the chase. Try to stop before your husky gets bored and wanders off to do his own thing.

Indestructible toys, such as Kongs, are good for your Siberian to play with when you are not available. By packing them tight with a variety of different tasty morsels every day, you will be providing your dog with a 'new' toy every day. He will, hopefully, spend lots of time trying to disgorge the contents of such toys and he will be well occupied when you are not there. Hard, plastic toys, such as the balls with holes in them that dispense biscuits when rolled around, are also enjoyed by huskies. Just make sure these sorts of toys are

indestructible. You will soon find out if they are not!

HOW DO DOGS LEARN?

It is not difficult to get inside your Siberian Husky's head and understand how he learns, as it is not dissimilar to the way we learn. Dogs learn by conditioning: they find out that specific behaviours produce specific consequences. This is known as operant conditioning or consequence learning. Consequences have to be immediate or clearly linked to the behaviour, as a dog sees the world in terms of action and result. Dogs will quickly learn if an action has a bad consequence or a good consequence.

Dogs also learn by association. This is known as classical conditioning or association learning. It is the type of learning made famous by Pavlov's experiment with dogs. Pavlov presented dogs with food and measured their salivary response (how much they drooled). Then he rang a bell just before presenting the food. At first, the dogs did not salivate until the food was presented. But after a while they learnt that the sound of the bell meant that food was coming and so they salivated when they heard the bell. A dog needs to learn the association in order for it to have any meaning. For example, a dog that has never seen a lead before will be completely indifferent to it. A dog that has learnt that a lead means he is going for a walk will get excited the second he sees the lead; he has learnt to associate a

lead with a walk. A dog that has been reprimanded by the whip of the lead may not like the lead at all or be ambivalent as to what it might signify.

BE POSITIVE
The most effective method of training dogs is to use their ability to learn by consequence and to teach that the behaviour you want produces a good consequence. For example, if you ask your Siberian Husky to "Sit" and reward him with a treat, he will learn that it is worth his while to sit on command because it will lead to a treat. He is far more likely to repeat the behaviour and the behaviour will become stronger, because it results in a positive outcome. This method of training is known as positive reinforcement and it generally leads to a happy, co-operative dog that is willing to work and a handler who has fun training their dog.

The opposite approach is negative reinforcement. This is far less effective and often results in a poor relationship between dog and owner. In this method of training, you ask your husky to "Sit" and if he does not respond, you deliver a sharp yank on the training collar or push his rear to the ground. The dog learns that not responding to your command has a bad consequence and he may be less likely to ignore you in the future. However, it may well have a bad consequence for you, too. A dog that is treated in this way may associate harsh handling with the handler and become aggressive or fearful. Instead of establishing a pattern of willing co-operation, you are establishing a relationship built on coercion.

This is very important to bear in mind when you are training a Siberian Husky; if he is subjected to harsh handling, he will almost certainly shut down and completely ignore you. A husky may give the impression that he is being stubborn and recalcitrant and you may be tempted to tell him off. However, it could be that he does not understand what you require of him and he is simply worried and unable to respond in the way you would like him to. If a husky is truly worried, scolding will make him even more worried and this is not the sort of relationship you would want with your dog. Show him what you require using the lure method, or ask him to do something he knows well and reward him to build up his confidence.

GETTING STARTED

As you train your Siberian Husky you will develop your own techniques as you get to know what motivates him. It does not matter what form of training you use, as long as it is based on positive methods.

There are a few important guidelines to bear in mind when you are training your husky:

• Find a training area that is free from distractions, particularly when you are just starting out. A Siberian Husky can lose focus quite easily, so it may be easier to train him indoors or in your garden to begin with.

Find a well-fenced area that is free from distractions so your husky will focus on you.

85

- Keep training sessions short, especially with young puppies that have very short attention spans.
- Do not train if you are in a bad mood or if you are on a tight schedule – the training session will be doomed to failure.
- If you are using a toy as a reward, make sure it is only available when you are training. In this way it has an added value for your husky.
- If you are using food treats, make sure they are bite-size and easy to swallow; you don't want to hang about while your husky chews on his treat. Dry biscuits or kibble will make him thirsty and again take longer to crunch through.
- Do not attempt to train your husky after he has eaten, or soon after returning from exercise. He will either be too full up to care about food treats or too tired to concentrate.
- When you are training, move around your allocated area so that your dog does not think that an exercise can only be performed in one place.
- If your husky is finding an exercise difficult, try not to get frustrated. Go back a step and praise him for his effort. You will probably find he is more successful when you try again at the next training session.
- If a training session is not going well – either because you are in the wrong frame of mind or the dog is not focusing – ask your husky to do something you know he

can do (such as a trick he enjoys performing) and then you can reward him with a food treat or a play with his favourite toy, ending the session on a happy, positive note.
- Do not train for too long. You need to end a training session on a high, with your husky wanting more, rather than making him sour by asking too much from him.

TRAINING EXERCISES

Husky puppies can be very food-motivated and you can get your pup to jump through hoops (literally) for a small piece of liver. This is very useful for instilling the basic commands.

Siberians should *never* be subjected to harsh handling or punitive methods. This is a breed that is tough but sensitive and a new Siberian Husky owner may misinterpret the signals they are getting. There is a tendency to think a Siberian is being naughty or stubborn whereas, in fact, the husky is worried and/or does not understand what is expected of him. A Siberian owner must learn what motivates his puppy and use this knowledge to get the best from him. A combination of tasty treats, fun play and lots of praise works well for most huskies. To begin with, keep distractions to a minimum so your husky can concentrate and them build them up gradually. Most important of all, train in short spells and finish before your husky gets bored.

THE SIT
This is the easiest exercise to teach, so it is rewarding for both you and your Siberian Husky.

- Choose a tasty treat and hold it just above your puppy's nose. As he looks up at the treat, he will naturally go into the 'Sit'. As soon as he is in position, reward him.
* Once he is doing this regularly, turn your lure into a handsignal and begin to add the "Sit" command. If your puppy does not immediately understand the handsignal, show him what is required by repeating the lure a few times.
- Repeat the exercise and when your pup understands what you want, introduce the "Sit" command.
- You can practise the Sit exercise at mealtimes by holding out the bowl and waiting for your dog to sit. Most huskies learn this one very quickly!

THE DOWN
Work hard at this exercise because a reliable 'Down' is useful in many different situations, and an instant 'Down' can be a lifesaver.

- Get your puppy in a Sit and put a treat on his nose and lower it between his paws, bringing it straight down from his chin and allow him to gnaw on it. If you bring the treat too far forward, he will get up. Sometimes nudging the treat in towards your puppy

Reward your husky as soon as he is in the correct position.

Use a treat to lure him into the Down.

slightly will make it minimally uncomfortable and this will elicit the Down position. Make sure the treat is tasty and wait for the right behaviour to happen. Remember to reward by relinquishing the treat as soon as your puppy's bottom has hit the deck.

- When your puppy is following the treat and going into position, introduce a handsignal, showing him what is required by returning to the lure signal if he does not understand. You may need to increase the value of your treats at this stage. Once your puppy is going into the position regularly, introduce the verbal command.
- Once your puppy is assuming

the Down position on the handsignal and verbal command you can build up this exercise over a period of time, each time waiting a little longer before giving the reward, so the puppy learns to stay in the Down.

THE RECALL
The Recall is fraught with difficulties and there are very, very few Siberian owners who can boast that their dog will reliably come back when let off the lead. It can be misleading, as Siberian Husky puppies may start off with a reasonably good recall. A puppy has a natural instinct to follow his mother and littermates, and this will be transferred to his new family with

a little encouragement. A husky is very responsive to vocal praise – and treats. So make yourself sound fun, and reward your husky when he comes to you in the house, or in the garden, and you will be building up a good association with the cue to "Come".

Do not make the mistake of becoming complacent and thinking that your Siberian Husky will repeat this behaviour when he is off lead in a new place. The moment you add distractions, such as an interesting scent, another dog, a rabbit, a bird or a squirrel, and you will almost certainly find your have 'lost' your husky. He will become focused on what he finds most interesting, and will

Do not neglect the Recall – even though your husky will need to be kept on a lead in public places.

ignore your calls. The problem with the Siberian is that all sense will desert him – and he will set off in pursuit of his new-found interest with absolutely no thought to the consequences. The chances are that he will disappear out of sight and it may take some time to find him or, worse still, he will run across a road and be involved in an accident. Tragically, all too many Siberian Huskies have lost their lives in this way.

Work on your Recall so you have a husky that responds happily and willingly at home – but the best advice is keep him on a lead when you are in public places.

WALKING ON A LOOSE LEAD
The Siberian Husky is bred to run ahead – but this does not mean that your husky cannot learn to walk on the lead in a civilised manner. Indeed, it is of paramount importance that he learns this lesson, as he will almost certainly spend more time on lead than the average pet dog.

In this exercise, as with all lessons that you teach your Siberian Husky, you must adopt a calm, consistent attitude. Your Siberian must learn that the only place to be is by your side, and he will be rewarded when he is in this position. Initially, you will need to use treats to lure him into position and to keep his attention focused on you but, in time, you will only need to reward him on a random basis. In this way, he will enjoy accompanying you wherever you take him.

- In the early stages of lead training pick a side and stick to it – do not be tempted to tighten the lead, as this will have the effect of making your husky want to pull against it.
- Get a handful of small tasty treats and use your 'lure' hand (which should be on the same side as your puppy) to lure your puppy into position by your side. Remove your lure hand away from your puppy's reach, say the command "Heel" or "Close", take one step, and if your pup is by your side, reward with a treat. Take another step and repeat the reward.
- Once this is going well, take two steps then reward and repeat again, and gradually build up the number of steps you can do with your husky by your side. Try not to do too much too soon.
- Keep your hands with the treats in out of your puppy's way so that he is not tempted to jump up for them. Always deliver the

The aim is to get your husky to walk on a loose lead.

reward quickly and by the side of your leg. If you get into the habit of rewarding in front of you, your puppy will anticipate this and start to walk in front of you and this may result in tripping you up!

- Remember to give lots of praise once your puppy is in the correct position.

- When your pup is walking alongside you, keep focusing his attention on you by talking to him and encouraging him, and then rewarding him when the lead is loose. Be unpredictable by changing direction, which will help to keep his attention.

- Do not attempt to take your puppy out on the lead until you have mastered the basics at home. You need to be confident that your puppy accepts the lead and will focus his attention on you, when requested, before you face the challenge of a busy environment.

- If you are heading somewhere special, such as to the park, the chances are your husky may pull ahead until the lead is tight. If this happens, stop in your tracks so that your puppy learns he cannot pull you everywhere he wants to go – husky puppies learn this very quickly. Vibrate the lead (don't yank!), call your puppy back, lure him to your side and start again. Eventually your puppy will learn that he cannot make progress until he is by your side. Only practise this when you have plenty of time!

STAYS

This may not be the most exciting exercise, but it is one of the most useful. Because of this you may wish to practise this when your husky has been well exercised and entertained, and is in the mood to learn. There are many occasions when you want your Siberian Husky to stay in position, even if it is only for a few seconds. The classic example is when you want your husky to stay in the back of the car until you have clipped on his lead. Some trainers use the verbal command "Stay" when the dog is to stay in position until your return to your dog and "Wait" if the dog is to stay in position for a few seconds until you give the next command. Others trainers use a universal "Stay" to cover all situations. It all comes down to personal preference, and as long as you are consistent, your dog will understand the command he is given.

It is good to teach your puppy, in the first instance, to stay until you return to him. In this way if he gets himself into a fix, he is more likely to wait for you rather than head off into the wide blue yonder.

• Ask your puppy for a 'Sit' or a 'Down' and use a handsignal (flat palm, facing the dog) and say "Stay" in a gentle, encouraging voice without staring too hard at your puppy, as this may make him want to move. Step a pace away from the dog. Wait a second, step back to your original position before your dog moves, and reward him. Gradually build up the number of steps you can do without your puppy moving. Always return to the front position before rewarding. If you reward your puppy while you are on the move, he may be more tempted to follow you.

* If he moves before you have stepped back, you are going too fast and you should return to fewer steps away so that you can always reward him for doing the right thing. He will soon learn that all he has to do is sit there until you return! If you have a lively pup, practise when he has been well exercised so that he is less likely to want to move away.

• Repeat the exercise, gradually increasing the

SOCIALISATION

While your Siberian Husky is mastering basic obedience exercises, there is other, equally important work to do with him. A Siberian is not only becoming a part of your home and family, he is becoming a member of the community.

Your Siberian Husky needs to be able to live in the outside world, coping calmly with every new situation that comes his way. It is your job to introduce him to as many different experiences as possible and to encourage him to behave in an appropriate manner.

In order to socialise your husky effectively, it is helpful to understand how his brain is developing and then you will get a perspective on how he sees the world.

CANINE SOCIALISATION
(Birth to 7 weeks)
This is the time when a dog learns how to be a dog. By interacting with his mother and his littermates, a young pup learns about leadership and submission. He learns to read body posture so that he understands the intentions of his mother and his siblings. A puppy that is taken away from his litter too early may

distance you can leave your dog. When you return to your dog's side, praise and reward him quietly and release him with a command, such as "OK".

- Remember to keep your body language very still when you are training this exercise and keep eye contact gentle and soft, rather than stern, so that you can give tacit encouragement to the still behaviour. Work on this exercise over a period of time and you will build up a really reliable Stay. Eventually you should proof the behaviour with more lively activity and surroundings.

With practice, your Siberian will be confident to stay while you are some distance away, but make sure you are in a safe, enclosed area.

always have behavioural problems with other dogs, either being fearful or aggressive.

Hopefully, your Siberian's breeder should have begun the socialisation period by introducing your future puppy to the sights and sounds of everyday life around the home, and to as many visitors as they can muster. Ideally, they will have carried your puppy out into the big wide world to be exposed to the sights of sounds of the great outdoors.

SOCIALISATION PERIOD
(7 to 12 weeks)
This is the time to expose a puppy to as many different experiences as possible. Your pup's breeder should start this process and you must continue it when the pup moves to his new home at eight weeks of age or older. This includes meeting different people, other dogs and animals, seeing new sights, and hearing a range of sounds, from the vacuum cleaner to the roar of traffic. A puppy learns very quickly and what he learns will stay with him for the rest of his life. This is the best time for a puppy to move to a new home, as he is adaptable and ready to form deep bonds.

FEAR-IMPRINT PERIOD
(8 to 11 weeks)

This occurs during the socialisation period and it can be the cause of problems if it is not handled carefully. If a pup is exposed to a frightening or painful experience, it will lead to lasting impressions. Obviously, you will attempt to avoid frightening situations, such as your pup being bullied by a mean-spirited older dog, or a firework going off, but you cannot always protect your puppy from the unexpected. If your pup has a nasty experience, the best plan is to make light of it and distract him by offering him a treat or a game. The pup will take the lead from you and will be reassured that there is nothing to worry about. If you mollycoddle him and sympathise with him, he is far more likely to retain the memory of his fear.

By exposing your puppy to all the things, usual and unusual, that he is likely to meet in his life in a positive fashion, he will gain confidence, which will help to offset any negative experiences. For instance, if your puppy has not met many people and has never met a man with a beard and the first bearded man he meets kicks him, he may develop concerns about men or specifically about men with beards. If he has already had lots of experience of people and men with beards, he is likely to bounce back from this one isolated, unpleasant experience.

SENIORITY PERIOD
(12 to 16 weeks)

During this period, your husky puppy starts to cut the apron strings and becomes more independent. He may become more challenging and less attentive to your commands. Bad habits, such as play biting, which may have been seen as endearing a few weeks earlier, should be discouraged but given an outlet with toy play and chew toys. Remember to use positive, reward-based training where you are a kind, consistent leader who helps and encourages your puppy to learn the right behaviour.

SECOND FEAR-IMPRINT
PERIOD (6 to 14 months)

This period is not as critical as the first fear-imprint period, but it should still be handled carefully. During this time your Siberian Husky may appear apprehensive, or he may show fear of something familiar. You may feel as if you have taken a backward step, but if you adopt a calm, positive manner, your husky will see that there is nothing to be frightened of. Do not make your dog confront the thing that frightens him. Simply distract his attention, and give him something else to think about, like obeying a simple command, such as "Sit" or

A puppy learns important lessons playing with his littermates.

"Down". This will give you the opportunity to praise and reward your dog and will help to boost his confidence. Give your puppy space away from the thing he is frightened of and, if it is safe to do so, give him plenty of time to approach or explore it to overcome his reticence.

YOUNG ADULTHOOD AND MATURITY (1 to 4 years)

The timing of this phase depends on the size of the dog: the bigger the dog, the later it is. This period coincides with a dog's increased size and strength, mental as well as physical. Some dogs will test their boundaries and both underlying fear and sexual competition may lead, in some cases, to aggression to other dogs. Consistency and continued training are essential at this time so that your Siberian Husky becomes a well-rounded member of the family pack.

IDEAS FOR SOCIALISATION

When you are socialising your Siberian, you want him to experience as many different situations as possible. Try out some of the following ideas, which will ensure your husky has an all-round education.

If you are taking on a rescued dog and have little knowledge of his background, it is important to work through a programme of socialisation. A young puppy soaks up new experiences like a sponge, but an older dog can still learn. If a rescued dog shows fear or apprehension, treat him in exactly the same way as you

would treat a youngster who is going through the second fear-imprint period.

- Accustom your husky to household noises, such as the vacuum cleaner, the television and the washing machine.
- Ask visitors to come to the door, wearing different types of clothing – for example, wearing a hat, a long raincoat, or carrying a stick or an umbrella.
- If you do not have children at home, make sure your Siberian Husky has a chance to meet and play with them. Go to a local park and watch children in the play area. You will not be able to

take your husky inside the play area, but he will see children playing and will get used to their shouts of excitement.
- Take a walk around some quiet streets, such as a residential area, so your husky can get used to the sound of traffic. As he becomes more confident, progress to busier areas. Remember, your lead is like a live wire and your feelings will travel directly to your Siberian Husky. Assume a calm, confident manner and your puppy will take the lead from you and have no reason to be fearful.

Socialise your young Siberian with other dogs of sound temperament.

- Go to a railway station. You don't have to get on a train if you don't need to, but your Siberian will have the chance to experience trains, people wheeling luggage, loudspeaker announcements and going up and down stairs and over railway bridges.
- If you live in the town, plan a trip to the country. You can enjoy a day out and provide an opportunity for your Siberian to see livestock, such as sheep, cattle and horses.
- One of the best places for socialising a dog is at a country fair. There will be crowds of people, livestock in pens, tractors, bouncy castles, fairground rides and food stalls. Make sure, however, that your puppy is not overwhelmed and give him plenty of time-outs away from the crowds.

THE ADOLESCENT SIBERIAN HUSKY

It happens to every dog – and every owner. One minute you have an obedient well-behaved youngster and the next you have a boisterous adolescent who appears to have forgotten everything he ever learnt.

A Siberian male will show adolescent behaviour at any time between 8-12 months. The first sign is that your husky will start

Take your Siberian out to events where he can meet dogs and people. These youngsters are attending their first rally.

to behave differently around dogs he previously played quite happily with. This is due to the amount of testosterone your adolescent Sibe is producing, which can be twice as much as an adult male dog. A youngster who showed respect to older dog suddenly becomes a young pretender, and older dogs may feel the need to teach him a lesson. In effect, the chemical changes taking place within your dog's body are turning him into a difficult teenager.

This can be a trying time, but it is important to retain a sense of perspective. Look at the situation from the dog's viewpoint and respond to uncharacteristic behaviour with firmness and consistency. Just like a teenager, an adolescent Siberian feels the need to flex his muscles and challenge the status quo. But if you provide a comprehensive programme of training, exercise and mental stimulation, (see page 90) and are quick to reward good behaviour, you will be able to channel his energies and earn his respect.

Female Siberian Huskies hit adolescence at any time from nine months and will usually have their first season at around this time. The hormonal changes may mean your husky becomes moody and quiet, although some become more playful and skittish. A

Adolescence can be a trying time...

female will be less tolerant of other females and keener to engage with male dogs. Post-season, many huskies show varying degrees of phantom pregnancy-type behavioural symptoms. In this state, a female may be protective of resources, such as food, potential nesting sites (e.g. beds, room corners, crates), and this may result in fights with other female dogs within the household. It is important to prevent this happening by ensuring the post-seasonal female has her own space where she feels secure, and supervising all situations regarding food and other resources to prevent squabbles breaking out.

As a responsible owner, it is your job to give your Siberian the tools to sail through this period of

change and emerge as a well-rounded and sociable member of the canine community. It is no coincidence that most dogs that are put up for rescue are at this age. It is because owners have not put in the early work and find themselves totally unable to cope with the behaviour of an adolescent dog.

It is also important to remember that adolescence can be highly individual, and it may be that you have a husky that shows no challenging or difficult behaviour and comes through this chapter of life without a care in the world. However, it is better to be prepared for what may happen!

WHEN THINGS GO WRONG
Positive, reward-based training has proved to be the most effective method of teaching dogs, but what happens when your Siberian Husky does something wrong and you need to show him that his behaviour is unacceptable? The old-fashioned school of dog training used to rely on the powers of punishment and negative reinforcement. A dog who raided the bin, for example, was smacked. Now we have learnt that it is not only unpleasant and cruel to hit a dog, it is also ineffective. If you hit a dog for stealing, he is more than likely to see you as the bad consequence of stealing, so he may raid the bin

again, but probably not when you are around. If he raided the bin some time before you discovered it, he will be even more confused by your punishment, as he will not relate your response to his 'crime'.

There are a number of strategies to tackle undesirable behaviour – and they have nothing to do with harsh handling.

Ignoring bad behaviour: The Siberian Husky is an intelligent dog, and it is understandable if he tries to influence a situation to his own advantage. For example, a young husky that barks when you are preparing his food, is showing his impatience and is attempting to train you, rather than the other way round. He believes he can

change a situation simply by making a noise – and even if he does not get his food any quicker, he is enjoying the attention he is getting when you shout at him to tell him to be quiet. He is still getting attention, and you are therefore probably rewarding the behaviour and encouraging him.

In this situation, the best and

TRAINING CLASSES

As soon as your puppy has been vaccinated and is able to mix with other dogs enrol him in a well-run puppy class. Your vet will have details of a local class.

Puppy classes are designed for pups between the ages of 11 to 20 weeks and give puppies a chance to play and interact together in a controlled, supervised environment. Siberian puppies generally excel in kind, gentle classes. Your puppy may occasionally sit under a chair for the first class, sizing up the rest of the puppies. However, once he has decided that puppy classes are a nice place to be, he will be keen to participate and work, especially for tasty food. If you can get his attention, he will pick things up promptly and perform them perfectly.

After completing puppy classes, you can graduate to a training club. Your vet will probably have details of clubs in your area, or you can ask friends who have dogs if they attend a club. Alternatively, use the internet to find out more information. But how do you know if the club is any good?

Before you take your dog, ask if you can go

to a class as an observer and find out the following:
- What experience does the instructor(s) have?
- Do they have experience with Siberian Huskies or, at least, with husky breeds? Do they show positive enthusiasm for spitz breeds or do they consider them untrainable?
- Is the class well organised and are the dogs reasonably quiet? A noisy class may indicate stressed puppies, which is not conducive to learning.
- Does the puppy class only contain puppies up to 20 weeks of age?
- Are there are a number of classes to suit dogs of different ages and abilities?
- Are positive, reward-based training methods used?
- Does the club train for the Good Citizen Scheme (see page 102)?

If you are not happy with the training club, find another one. An inexperienced instructor who cannot handle a number of dogs in a confined environment can do more harm than good.

most effective response is to ignore him. Suspend food preparations and get on with another task, such as washing up. Do not go near the food or the food bowl again until your husky is calm and quiet. Repeat this on every occasion when your husky barks and he will soon learn that barking is non-productive. He is not rewarded with your attention – or with getting food. It will not take long for him to realise that being quiet is the most effective strategy.

Stopping bad behaviour:
Prevention is always better than cure and it is much more motivating to set your puppy up for success rather than coming down on him like a ton of bricks. Try to minimise opportunities for mischievous behaviour. For example, do not allow him unsupervised in the sitting room if he is likely to jump on the sofa, or in the kitchen if he is likely to raid the rubbish bin, and, where possible, interrupt undesirable behaviour by teaching an alternative. Call him to you in bright, happy voice – using a stern voice will put a negative slant on the situation, which will make your Siberian worried, and therefore uncooperative. If necessary, you can attract him with a toy or a treat. The moment your Siberian stops the undesirable behaviour and comes towards you, you can reward his good behaviour. You can back this up by running through a couple of simple exercises, such

as a 'Sit' or a 'Down', and rewarding with treats. In this way, your husky focuses his attention on you and sees you as the greatest source of reward and pleasure.

PROBLEM BEHAVIOUR

If you have trained your Siberian Husky from puppyhood, survived his adolescence and established yourself as a fair and consistent leader, you will end up with a brilliant companion dog. The Siberian is a well- balanced dog, who rarely has hang-ups if he has been correctly reared and socialised.

DESTRUCTIVE BEHAVIOUR

The Siberian Husky has a reputation for being destructive – pages on websites are devoted to the havoc that has been wreaked from ripped-up sofas and curtains to chewed-up doors and skirting boards. However, the cause and the solution are both simple and straightforward.

A bored husky is a destructive husky. This breed is mentally active and requires stimulation. If this is lacking, a husky will be quick to find his own agenda. Coupled with this, a Siberian Husky is bred to run for miles and he needs to channel his energy. Extensive varied exercise, coupled with the opportunity to use his brain, will – nine times out of ten – stop a husky from being destructive.

Do not make the mistake of getting angry with your Siberian when you return home to find he

Set ground rules. There will be times when you need to call an instant halt to your dog's behaviour.

has been on the rampage. It will only mean that he is more likely to rip up your furnishings when you are not there, which will only compound the problem. Indoor crates can sometimes be overused and it is often preferable to pen a puppy off in a room so he can still move about etc. The use of an indoor crate and providing plenty of chewing opportunities with appropriate toys and chews will also help to prevent domestic damage. However, providing stimulation and exercise are the essential ingredients in solving this problem – a tired, contented dog is far less likely to look for mischief.

The Siberian is geared to living in a pack and may become anxious if he has to cope on his own.

Getting up on to the sofa or your favourite armchair and growling when you tell him to get back on the floor.

To stop this happening, prevent your puppy from getting up on the sofa by supervising him at all times, denying access to the room unsupervised or putting something on the sofa that prevents your puppy from getting on it. Make sure all the interesting things go on at floor level; interact and play with your puppy at floor level to lower his interest in getting on the sofa. Put a houseline (a long, light lead without a handle) on your dog's collar so he can trail it around the house (ensure you are always supervising your dog wearing this). If your puppy gets on the sofa, pick up the end of the houseline and, without looking at your puppy, gently vibrate the lead and guide your puppy off without interacting with your dog. Reward behaviour off the sofa. In this way you are not getting into a physical conflict with your puppy; you are showing him that you are not interested in the sofa and that more interesting things happen on the ground!

Becoming possessive over a toy, or guarding his food bowl by growling when you (or another dog) get too close.

From a puppy, get your husky used to being rewarded for handing you toys. Play with a toy he likes, but keep his favourite toy so that you can swap the toy for his favourite, so you are always rewarding this behaviour – that is,

In some cases, a Siberian Husky may resort to destructive behaviour because he is suffering from separation anxiety (see below). If you are uncertain as to the cause of your husky's behaviour and feel out of your depth, do not delay in seeking professional help. This is readily available, usually through a referral from your vet, or you can find out additional information on the internet (see Appendices for web addresses). An animal behaviourist will have experience in tackling problem behaviour and will be able to help both you and your dog.

RESOURCE GUARDING

Some Siberians can show resource-guarding behaviour. This may take a number of different forms and it may be directed towards you and your family, or towards other dogs in the same household. Typical resource guarding includes:

SEPARATION ANXIETY

A Siberian Husky should be brought up to accept short periods of separation from his owner so that he does not become anxious. A new puppy should be left for short periods on his own, ideally in a safe place where he cannot get up to any mischief. It is a good idea to leave him with a boredom-busting toy so he will be happily occupied in your absence. When you return, do not make a huge fuss. Wait a few moments, and then calmly go to your dog, telling him how good he has been. If this scenario is repeated a number of times, your Siberian will soon learn that being left on his own is no big deal.

Problems with separation anxiety are most likely to arise if you take on a rescued dog who has major insecurities. You may also find your husky hates being left if you have failed to accustom him to short periods of isolation when he was growing up. Separation anxiety is expressed in a number of ways and all are equally distressing for both dog and owner. An anxious dog who is left alone may bark and whine continuously, urinate and defecate, and may be extremely destructive.

There are a number of steps you can take when attempting to solve this problem.

- Put up a baby-gate between adjoining rooms; leave your dog in one room while you are in the other room. Your dog will be able to see you and hear you, but he is learning to cope without being right next to you. Build up the amount of time you can leave your dog in easy stages. Then you can build up to being out of sight and then out of hearing. Always return to your dog before he gets distressed. At the start, this may be for only a few seconds, but you can gradually build up the time.
- Buy some boredom-busting toys and fill them with some tasty treats. Whenever you leave your dog, give him a food-filled toy so that he is busy while you are away.
- If you decide to use a crate, make sure it is cosy and train your husky to get used to going in his crate while you are in the same room - without locking him in it. Feed him in his crate and give him chews and toys in his crate so that he builds up positive associations. Gradually build up the amount of time he spends in the crate and then start leaving the room for short periods. When you return, do not make a fuss of your dog. Leave him for five or ten minutes before releasing him, so that he gets used to your comings and goings. Get him happy with going in and out of the crate before shutting him in. Shutting a husky puppy against his will in a crate can be harmful. They can scratch, paw and bite at the crate until they really hurt themselves, to say nothing of the distress.
- Pretend to go out, putting on your coat and jangling keys, but do not leave the house. An anxious dog often becomes hyped up by the ritual of leaving and this will help to desensitise him.
- When you go out, leave a radio or a TV on. Some dogs are comforted by hearing voices and background noise when they are left alone.
- Sacrifice an old piece of clothing that he can use for bedding. Having the smell of you may help to calm him (remember to replenish the smell on a regular basis!).
- Try to make your absences as short as possible when you are first training your dog to accept being on his own.

If you take these steps, your dog should become less anxious and, over a period of time, you should be able to solve the problem. However, if you are failing to make progress, do not delay in calling in expert help.

if you give me this, you will get something better. Swap toys for treats. Do not physically remove the toy from your dog's mouth but wait until he drops it by you and then reward well. If your dog brings you a toy, do not always take it from him. Simply pet him while he has it in his mouth and say what a good boy he is. In this way he will enjoy giving you the toys and will have no reason to become possessive around toys because you always provide something equally as nice or better.

Do not allow your Siberian to make his own rules…

To prevent food bowl guarding, follow these instructions and you will not have a problem in later life. If your dog already has a bowl-guarding problem, consult a behaviourist to help you solve it. *Never* confront your husky when he is eating if he growls at you or starts to eat manically fast as you approach. Seek expert advice.

When your puppy is eating, get in the habit of stroking him on his back to accustom him to your proximity. While he is eating put something very tasty from your hand into his bowl. In this way he will associate hands around food bowls as a positive thing. While your puppy is eating, offer a tasty morsel (of a higher value than he has in his bowl). If your puppy leaves the bowl voluntarily, give him the treat and while he is eating it, lift the bowl up and then return the bowl to the puppy. He will associate people coming towards his bowl as a good thing rather than worrying that his resource is going to be taken away.

Finally, as your puppy is eating, put your hand in the bowl and offer a tasty treat. By doing this at every meal time, your puppy will not grow to be possessive and will not feel the need to guard.

Do not follow this programme with a dog who is already showing food-bowl aggression. Seek expert help.

If your puppy is guarding his food bowl from other dogs, feed all dogs separately so that each has enough space to finish his food without the worry of other dogs stealing his ration.

Growling when a dog or person approaches his bed or gets too close to where he is lying.
Start by getting your puppy used to being handled all over so that he is not sensitive to being touched and handled. Remember that a sleeping dog who is suddenly touched may react on the spur of the moment, so ensure you do not approach a sleeping dog without making a noise to wake him first. It is important to let your dog have a safe place away from the hurly burly of life and you should respect his space. If you need him to move, call him away from his place and to you, then reward him for doing so.

When your puppy is relaxed, get him used to being handled in his bed and getting lots of rewards so that he views people in his space as a great thing. If you have lots of visitors and a busy household, ensure your dog has a safe haven he can retreat to, so he is not bothered by people or young children. Make sure everyone in the house knows not to disturb your puppy while he is sleeping so that his bed is his safe haven. Obviously, if your dog already has problems around his personal space, you will need to get expert help.

In each of these scenarios, the Siberian has something he values and he aims to keep it. He may have been brought up in a competitive litter where interesting resources were thin on the ground and food was limited because all puppies were fed from the same bowl. Some dogs may just be possessive.

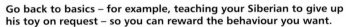
Go back to basics – for example, teaching your Siberian to give up his toy on request – so you can reward the behaviour you want.

Prevention and consistency is the best way to tackle this problem. If you see signs of your husky guarding what he sees as 'valuable' resources, you must work at lowering the value of what is being guarded and instilling your dog with confidence about sharing. Although you need to be consistent, you also need to use positive training methods so that your husky is rewarded for the behaviour you want. In this way, his 'correct' behaviour will be strengthened and repeated.

The golden rule is not to become confrontational. The dog will see this as a challenge and may become even more determined not to co-operate.

There are a number of steps you can take to manipulate your puppy to do your bidding without resorting to human aggression. They are far more likely to have a successful outcome. They include:

• Go back to basics and hold daily training sessions. Make sure you have some really tasty treats and run through all the training exercises you have taught your Siberian. Remember, boredom is very often the key to undesirable behaviour. By giving him things to do, you are providing mental stimulation and you have the opportunity to make a big fuss of him and reward him when he does well. This will help to reinforce the message that you are the leader and that it is rewarding to do as you ask.

• Teach your Siberian something new. This can be as simple as learning a trick, such as shaking paws. Having something new to think about will mentally stimulate your husky and he will benefit from interacting with you.

• Be 100 per cent consistent with all house rules – if you do not want your husky on the sofa, then prevent this happening.

• If your husky becomes possessive over toys follow the simple measures on page 98.

• Teach your Siberian not to

barge through doors ahead of you or leap from the back of the car before you release him. You may need to put your dog on the lead and teach him to "Wait" at doorways and then reward him for letting you go through first.

If your Siberian husky is progressing well with his retraining programme, think about getting involved with a dog sport, such as agility or canicross (see page 105). This will give your husky a positive outlet for his energies.

NEW CHALLENGES

If you enjoy training your Siberian Husky, you may want to try one of the many dog sports that are now on offer.

GOOD CITIZEN SCHEME

This is a scheme run by the Kennel Club in the UK and the American Kennel Club in the USA. The schemes promote responsible ownership and help you to train a well-behaved dog that will fit in with the community. The schemes are excellent for all pet owners and they are also a good starting point if you plan to compete with your Siberian Husky when he is older.

The KC and the AKC schemes vary in format. In the UK there are three levels: bronze, silver and gold, with each test becoming progressively more demanding. In the AKC scheme there is a single test.

AGGRESSION

Aggression is a complex issue, as there are different causes and the behaviour may be triggered by numerous factors. It may be directed towards people, but far more commonly it is directed towards other dogs. Aggression in dogs may be the result of:
- Resource guarding (see page 100).
- Defensive behaviour: This may be induced by fear, pain or punishment.
- Territory: A dog may become aggressive if strange dogs or people enter his territory (which is generally seen as the house and garden).
- Intra-sexual issues: This is aggression between sexes – male-to-male or female-to-female.
- Parental instinct: A mother dog may become aggressive if she is protecting her puppies.

Siberian Huskies are not generally aggressive, but lack of experience with other breeds may lead to anxiety, which can develop into aggressive behaviour towards other dogs as the Siberian reaches maturity. Female huskies will generally react better to male dogs, and male huskies will get on better with female dogs. Most huskies prefer to avoid confrontation and it is important that husky owners socialise their dogs from puppyhood by getting them to meet other unthreatening puppies, calm, older dogs and by avoiding negative experiences. It is easy for a new owner to miss that a husky puppy is scared or worried, as they seem such hardy little souls. However, a frightening encounter (such as being bowled over by an over-enthusiastic dog or being chased by a lively youngster) will have a huge impact on the husky psyche, which he will not forget.

Some huskies will learn to avoid other dogs in future, but others will react by being confrontational. This can escalate with each negative encounter and result in an aggressive dog. This is usually the result of fear, so proper

Some of the exercises include:
- Walking on a loose lead among people and other dogs.
- Recall amid distractions.
- A controlled greeting where dogs stay under control while their owners meet.
- The dog allows all-over grooming and handling by his owner, and also accepts being handled by the examiner.
- Stays, with the owner in sight and then out of sight.
- Food manners, allowing the owner to eat without begging and taking a treat on command.
- Sendaway – sending the dog to his bed.

The tests are designed to show the control you have over your dog and his ability to respond correctly and remain calm in all situations. The Good Citizen Scheme is taught at most training clubs. For more information, log on to the Kennel Club or AKC website (see Appendices).

SHOWING

In your eyes, your Siberian Husky is the most beautiful dog in the world – but would a judge agree? Showing is a highly competitive sport and the Siberian is drawing increasingly big entries. However, many owners get bitten by the showing bug, and their calendar is governed by the dates of the top showing fixtures.

To be successful in the show ring, a Siberian Husky must conform as closely as possible to the Breed Standard, which is a

socialisation with the right sort of dogs – and with lots of different breeds – should clearly be high on any husky owner's list of priorities.

Overly rough play with other dogs should be avoided; careful supervised encounters should be encouraged. Huskies do like rough and tumble on their terms but any overtly physical play should be gently interrupted at every turn, using suitable distraction techniques with toys, treats and praise to get the behaviour you want.

If you have taken on a rescued dog that has been poorly socialised, you can try to make up for lost time and work with other dogs of sound temperament in controlled situations. However, if you are concerned about your dog's behaviour, you would be well advised to call in professional help. If the aggression is directed towards people, you should seek immediate advice. This behaviour can escalate very quickly and could have disastrous consequences.

Try to avoid excessively rough play with other dogs.

The Siberian is more than capable of earning Good Citizen awards. This UK puppy gained her bronze and silver when she was six months old and her gold aged just seven months and a week.

written blueprint describing the 'perfect' dog (see Chapter Seven). To get started you need to buy a puppy that has show potential and then train him to perform in the ring. A Siberian will be expected to stand in show pose, gait for the judge in order to show off his natural movement, and to be examined by the judge. This involves a detailed hands-on examination, so your husky must be bombproof when handled by strangers.

Many training clubs hold ringcraft classes, which are run by experienced showgoers. At these classes, you will learn how to handle your Siberian in the ring, and you will also find out about rules, procedures and show ring etiquette.

The best plan is to start off at some small, informal shows where you can practise and learn the tricks of the trade before graduating to bigger shows. It's a long haul starting in the very first puppy class, but the dream is to make your Siberian Husky into a Champion.

COMPETITIVE OBEDIENCE

The Siberian Husky is not a natural when it comes to competitive obedience – in many ways he is too intelligent, and too keen on his own ideas, to give his full co-operation, However, some owners, particularly in the US,

have achieved a fair degree of success. There are various levels of achievement and, as you progress, the amount of encouragement and support you can give in terms of praise and verbal cues diminishes. Accuracy is the top priority and marks are lost for even the slightest crooked angle noticed when the dog is sitting. If a dog is momentarily distracted or works too far away from his owner in heelwork, again points will be deducted.

The exercises that must be mastered include the following:

- **Heelwork:** Dog and handler must complete a set pattern on and off the lead, which includes left turns, right turns, about turns and changes of pace.
- **Recall:** This may be when the handler is stationary or on the move.
- **Retrieve:** This may be a dumbbell or any article chosen by the judge.
- **Sendaway:** The dog is sent to a designated spot and must go into an instant 'Down' until he is recalled by the handler.
- **Stays:** The dog must stay in the 'Sit' and in the 'Down' for a set amount of time. In advanced classes, the handler is out of sight.
- **Scent:** The dog must retrieve a single cloth from a pre-arranged pattern of cloths that has his owner's scent, or in advanced classes, the judge's scent. There may also be decoy cloths.
- **Distance control:** The dog must execute a series of moves ('Sit', 'Stand', 'Down') without

leaving his position and with the handler at a distance.

Even though competitive obedience requires accuracy and precision, if you decide to have a go, ensure you make it fun for your Siberian, with lots of praise and rewards so that you motivate him to do his best. Many training clubs run advanced classes for those who want to compete in obedience, or you can hire the services of a professional trainer for one-on-one sessions.

AGILITY

This fun sport has grown enormously in popularity over the past few years and the Siberian Husky, when fully motivated, is an enthusiastic competitor. If you want to get involved in agility, you need good control over your Siberian to keep him focused on the equipment as, obviously, he must be off the lead. You also need to keep your husky fit and at the correct weight.

In agility competitions, each dog must complete a set course over a series of obstacles, which include:
• Jumps (upright hurdles and long jump, varying in height – small, medium and large – depending on the size of the dog)
• Weaves
• A-frame
• Dog walk
• Seesaw
• Tunnels (collapsible and rigid)
• Tyre

Dogs may compete in Jumping classes, with jumps, tunnels and

If you want to get involved in showing, you will need to learn how to exhibit your Siberian in the ring.

weaves, or in Agility classes, which have the full set of equipment. Faults are awarded for poles down on the jumps, missed contact points on the A-frame, dog walk and seesaw, and refusals. If a dog takes the wrong course, he is eliminated. The winner is the dog that completes the course in the fastest time with no faults. As you progress up the levels, courses become progressively harder with more twists, turns and changes of direction.

If you want to get involved in agility, you will need to find a club that specialises in the sport (see Appendices). You will not be allowed to start training until your

Siberian Husky is 12 months old and you cannot compete until he is 18 months old. This rule is for the protection of the dog, who may suffer injury if he puts strain on bones and joints while he is still growing.

CANICROSS

Canicross is a great sport where you and your dog engage in a shared activity, which you both thoroughly enjoy. Basically, the sport involves cross-country running attached to your dog. Dogs must be 12 months of age to compete, but you can gradually build up training from about nine months as long as you are careful not to overdo it, as too much

The athletic Siberian enjoys the challenge of agility.

exercise in a growing dog can put pressure on developing joints and cause problems later on.

Competitors wear a waist belt, which attaches via a bungee line to their dog in a padded, well-fitted harness. It is not usually hard to train your husky to go out in front and is a brilliant excuse to get out into the countryside. You can also exercise your dog's mental powers by teaching him directional commands for super-smooth running! Huskies enjoy exploring, relish exercise and soon pick up the left ("haw") and right ("gee") commands involved in the sport and it helps them build their confidence. Many owners just let their dogs do their own thing, but canicross will help you bond and connect with your dog in a different way.

Canicross is the perfect way for you and your Siberian to stay fit and healthy.

SCOOTERING/BIKEJORING
This involves your Siberian Husky pulling you on a scooter or a bicycle. It is not for the faint-hearted, but it can be fast and furious as well as great fun. It is necessary to have your husky well trained before you start this, so that at least you can slow him down and stop him when necessary. You and your dog's safety is paramount, so you must ensure that you keep your line from the bike to the dog tight so that there is never any danger of running your dog over. An accident or even just a scare early on can so traumatise your husky that he will never want to go near your bike or scooter again. Do

not overdo any exercise and only gradually build up the distances you go. You will also need to ensure the safety of other passers-by!

SKIJORING
In this sport, you go skiing attached to your dog. If you are already an adept skier with excellent ability, you may like to join up with your dog and do it together. What could be better than seeing a husky work on snow in this way?

MUSHING
This is the obvious choice for a husky owner. Two or more huskies are attached to either a

sled, if you are lucky enough to have regular snowfalls, or to a wheeled 'rig' for off-season training or more temperate climates that do not get much snow. Competitions take place during the winter where you and your dogs run a timed course along a marked set trail of varying distances.

In the UK where most races are 'dryland' races (i.e. not on snow unless you are lucky) course length can vary from around one to five miles and will often be dictated by trail conditions and temperature. Where the temperature and trail conditions allow, rallies may be longer and more challenging. Endurance competitions over snow, such as the Iditarod and Yukon Quest, take place in the United States and Canada over many miles, with large teams of eight or more huskies. This may well be something most husky owners can only dream of!

Competing in shorter races every winter can mean a lot of early morning training when it is still dark, as well as early weekend mornings travelling to distant parts of the country to take part in rallies. These are brilliant, competitive but fun events where you can meet like-minded husky owners, get tips on looking after your dogs from more experienced mushers and get involved in the welcoming Siberian community.

It is a good idea to attend a local husky rally before you get your dog so you can see if the sport and breed is really for you. Siberian owners are passionate about their breed and free with advice and knowledge to those people who genuinely want to learn more and do the right thing for their husky. You will get lots of useful information by meeting

Fast and furious, bikejoring requires a high level of control.

existing husky owners who are more than willing to give you a 'warts and all' picture of husky ownership!

Once you are decided that mushing huskies is the sport for you, do not forget that you cannot just take to the highway with your dogs – indeed, you would be committing an offence. Local authorities and forestry commissions will generally have a 'permit' system that allows you access to trails for an annual fee. If

you are lucky, some private landowners may allow you to run your dogs on their land, but these are few and far between. Where demands on public and private land is growing and becoming more prohibitive due to wildlife, conservation and public amenity concerns, this can be a difficult aspect of your venture so you should explore this carefully in your local area if you plan to race your huskies. If you start running your dogs without permission, you may be breaking the law and, in addition, run the risk of annoying the authorities, who may decide to withdraw permits for other mushers and thus ruin the facility for other husky owners.

GETTING STARTED

Mushing your dogs is a fantastic, thrilling and stimulating sport that both you and your huskies will love, but you will need to train your dogs carefully. Get advice and help from experienced mushers, who can advise you on kit, equipment and caring for your husky athlete.

Mushing requires at least two huskies, but do not take on two husky puppies at the same time. It is usually a recipe for disaster as

Mushing soon becomes the most addictive of sports.

they are likely to bond with each other instead of with you. When two puppies are brought up together, you may get a less confident puppy relying on the more confident puppy in interactions with people and with other dogs. So if you do get two dogs at the same time, you will need to take them out and train them separately. I would always advise getting one puppy first followed by another dog a year or two later.

If you want to work your dog, hopefully you will have met a knowledgeable breeder at rallies, bought a puppy from them and have all the after-sales help that

you need. Ideally, you will be able to find a mentor locally, and go to one of the teach-ins held by various clubs, or an "urban mushing clinic" in the US. This is because you can look at the various designs of scooters and rigs, to see what suits you before you commit to spending too much money. You will also be told the requirements of equipment for running with the clubs – some of the home-made "training" rigs that appear for sale on the Internet do not meet the safety rules for running with any organisations. Some are downright dangerous for you and your dogs.

Dogs cannot run in races until they are 12 months old, but you can start introducing them to pulling something very light, that they can barely feel the weight of, at around 6-8 months. Build up distances slowly, and always go at the pace your dog is happy with.

You will need a properly measured and fitted running harness, such as an "h-back" or "x-back", as using an ordinary walking harness will mean the dog is putting pressure on the wrong areas of its body and risking injury. Harnesses, collars and other equipment must be at least triple stitched with special thread to reduce the risk of failure.

Dog teams need to be evenly matched for ability and enthusiasm, and all of them should be happy with what they are doing.

Joining a club with third party insurance for working your dogs, or arranging your own, is essential. Most landowners will not give you permission to run your dogs on their land without it.

Teach your dog the commands on walks - "gee" for right, "haw" for left and "on by" or "leave it" for loose dogs/rabbits/squirrels/skunks, depending on where you live!

Although you can start working with one dog on a bike, or purpose-made scooter, or by cani-crossing, dogs seem to learn better by watching other dogs doing it. If you have tried to teach them not to pull on walks, they may need the initial motivation of another team to chase.

This is where group training can come in very handy when you are just starting out. It will also get your dog used to the conditions of a rally in miniature, which may otherwise be quite overpowering for them the first time if you always train alone. It can also help teach your dogs to pass or be passed on the trail, without panicking, fighting, or jumping into the middle of the other team for a play!

Dog teams need to be evenly matched for both ability and enthusiasm, or one dog may end up being dragged and put off for life. If someone offers you the chance to try your dog with theirs, make sure it is a calm, older dog that isn't going to go off like a rocket.

Do not run more than one or two dogs on a bike or scooter. Rigs are much more stable and

The Siberian Husky is a challenging breed to own, but if you put in the time and effort, you will be rewarded with an outstanding companion.

safer for both you and the dogs. Do not run on tarmac – it will damage your dog's joints, and this may not become apparent until it is too late.

Some dogs can overheat surprisingly quickly, even when it feels cold to you. Humidity is an extra complication – it is harder for dogs to dissipate heat if the air around them is full of moisture. Always take plenty of water, and it is best not to run if the temperature is above 12 C. The most important rule of mushing is that all your dogs should be happy with what they are doing, and all your lines should be tight. If they aren't, use your brakes until they are. Scooting *past* your team is not the object of the exercise!

Never yell at your dogs; it doesn't make them run any faster. Eventually they just tune you out and don't listen to any of your commands. There's an old musher's saying - "you can't push rope" If your dog is not out in front pulling, you need to go back to training basics or get some help.

SUMMING UP
The Siberian Husky is an outstanding companion dog – and once you have owned one, no other breed will do. He is intelligent, fun loving and affectionate, and when you give him a job to do that he relishes, he is an eager and willing worker.

Make sure that you keep your half of the bargain: spend time socialising and training your Siberian Husky so that you can be proud to take him anywhere and he will always be a credit to you.

THE PERFECT SIBERIAN HUSKY

Chapter 7

All Siberian Huskies should be immediately recognisable as a member of that breed and no other. The Breed Standard acts as a blueprint by describing those characteristics that distinguish the Siberian Husky from all other breeds. It should also detail the structure and proportions required to enable a Siberian Husky to perform its original function. These descriptions are an important source of reference to breeders and judges who wish to preserve the breed and avoid a gradual alteration in appearance.

Kennel clubs around the world have different formats for their Standards. The written descriptions of the Siberian Husky are broadly similar but may differ in some details. In this chapter we will look at the American Kennel Club (AKC) Standard and the Kennel Club (UK) Standard. The FCI Standard, used in Europe and other countries, is virtually identical to the AKC Standard.

FIT FOR FUNCTION
Since January 2009, all UK Kennel Club Breed Standards have the following opening paragraph:

A Breed Standard is the guideline which describes the ideal characteristics, temperament and appearance of a breed and ensures that the breed is fit for function. Absolute soundness is essential. Breeders and judges should at all times be careful to avoid obvious conditions or exaggerations which would be detrimental in any way to the health, welfare or soundness of this breed. From time to time certain conditions or exaggerations may be considered to have the potential to affect dogs in some breeds adversely, and judges and breeders are requested to refer to the Kennel Club website for details of any such current issues. If a feature or quality is desirable it should only be present in the right measure.

The Kennel Club is keen to promote pedigree dogs that are fit and healthy and able to perform their original function without stress or injury. Luckily, the Siberian Husky is an unexaggerated breed. Therefore, provided correct leg length and angulation are selected, along with the correct ribcage and spine, he should have no problem performing as a sled dog. Judges and breeders should also select for those characteristics that enable survival in Siberian conditions described in the rest of the Standard, as these will distinguish the Siberian Husky from other sled-dog breeds and crossbreeds.

The Siberian Husky must be fit for function, with a construction that allows him to do the work he was designed for.

ANALYSIS AND INTERPRETATION

Depending on the Breed Standard and on gender, the Siberian Husky can vary in height from 20 inches (51 cm to 23.5 inches (60 cm). Not only that, the breed can come in any colour and any coat markings, though some are more frequently seen than others. There is also room for some variation in coat length. When confronted by a number of Siberian Huskies, none of them identical, it is easy to see why some people think they are difficult to judge and "vary too much"! Those of us who love them cherish their individuality. No one else's Siberian will look exactly like yours.

However, there are limits to the variation that can be allowed, otherwise we would lose the specific characteristics that make

the Siberian Husky the fastest purebred sled dog in existence and still capable of surviving a Siberian winter.

Let us look at each part of the dog in detail.

GENERAL APPEARANCE AND CHARACTERISTICS
AKC

The Siberian Husky is a medium-sized working dog, quick and light on his feet and free and graceful in action. His moderately compact and well furred body, erect ears and brush tail suggest his Northern heritage. His characteristic gait is smooth and seemingly effortless. He performs his original function in harness most capably, carrying a light load at a moderate speed over great distances. His body proportions and form reflect this basic balance of power, speed and endurance. The males of the

Siberian Husky breed are masculine but never coarse; the bitches are feminine but without weakness of structure. In proper condition, with muscle firm and well developed, the Siberian Husky does not carry excess weight.

KC

Medium-sized working sled-dog, quick and light on feet. Free and graceful in action, with well furred body, erect ears and brush tail. Proportions reflect a basic balance of power, speed and endurance, never appearing so heavy or coarse as to suggest a freighting animal, nor so light and fragile as to suggest a sprint-racing animal. Males are masculine but never coarse, bitches feminine but without weakness of structure. Muscle firm and well developed, no excess weight.

Characteristics: Medium size, moderate bone, well balanced proportions, ease and freedom of movement, and good disposition.

You can see that the Siberian Husky travels great distances at a moderate speed, pulling a light load. In practice the distances covered can be as much as 30-50 miles (48-80 km) per day with each dog pulling on average two to three times his own bodyweight. Moderate speed for dogs working like this varies from a lope to a fast trot.

Great value is placed on the efficiency and soundness of the dog's movement, otherwise he would tire too easily and be prone to injury. Correct Siberian Huskies do not resemble small Alaskan Malamutes (a freighting breed). In correct condition, the Siberian Husky has lean, hard muscle and with his dense fur to keep him warm, there is little fat on the ribcage.

British Breed Record Holder Ch. Forstal's Kaliznik. Cubby, as he was known, won 40 CCs, 32 BOBs and 23 RCCs, winning two Working Groups. He was an influential sire, fathering six Champions, and an enthusiastic and hard-working sled dog.

TEMPERAMENT
AKC
The characteristic temperament of the Siberian Husky is friendly and gentle, but also alert and outgoing. He does not display the possessive qualities of the guard dog, nor is he overly suspicious of strangers or aggressive with other dogs. Some measure of reserve and dignity may be expected in the mature dog. His intelligence, tractability, and eager disposition make him an agreeable companion and willing worker.

KC
Friendly and gentle, alert and outgoing. Does not display traits of the guard dog, not suspicious with strangers or aggressive with dogs but some measure of reserve expected in mature dog. Intelligent, tractable and eager disposition. An agreeable companion and willing worker.

Do not buy a Siberian Husky if you want a dog that barks at intruders. The typical Siberian will merely regard a burglar as a visiting entertainer and is unlikely to utter a sound – except maybe to howl mournfully when he leaves with your valuables in a sack! In a mixed group of dogs the Siberian Husky is rarely an aggressor, using instead a subtle mix of body language to exert leadership. While willing to work, the Siberian's intelligence is not easily turned to obedience. Indeed, they are notorious for disobeying recall commands. A Siberian is clever enough to co-operate with you when it suits him, but he can easily identify situations when disobedience serves his own purpose better!

HEAD AND SKULL
AKC

Skull: Of medium size and in proportion to the body; slightly rounded on top and tapering from the widest point to the eyes. Faults: Head clumsy or heavy; head too finely chiseled. Stop: The stop is well-defined and the bridge of the nose is straight from the stop to the tip. Fault: Insufficient stop. Muzzle: Of medium length; that is, the distance from the tip of the nose to the stop is equal to the distance from the stop to the occiput. The muzzle is of medium width, tapering gradually to the nose, with the tip neither pointed nor square. Faults: Muzzle either too snipy or too coarse; muzzle too short or too long. Nose: Black in gray, tan or black dogs; liver in copper dogs; may be flesh-colored in pure white dogs. The pink-streaked "snow nose" is acceptable.

KC

Medium size in proportion to the body, presents a finely chiselled fox-like appearance. Slightly rounded on top, tapering gradually from widest point to eyes. Muzzle medium length and width, neither snipy nor coarse, tapering gradually to rounded nose. Tip of nose to stop equidistant from stop to occiput. Stop clearly defined but not excessive. Line of the nose straight from the stop to tip. Nose black in grey, tan or black dogs; liver in copper dogs; and may be flesh-coloured in pure white. In winter, pink-streaked 'snow nose' is acceptable.

The Standards agree on the general proportions and shape of the head and muzzle and Siberians should have a muzzle that is equal in length to the cranium. This is an unexaggerated ratio, which promotes a natural appearance and allows room in both upper and lower jaws for a good set of teeth. The KC Standard specifies that the head should have a "finely chiselled fox-like appearance" as does the Canadian Standard, but this is omitted from the AKC and FCI Standards. This can result in Siberians from different bloodlines having somewhat different heads. This is acceptable so long as they do not give the impression of belonging to another breed.

EYES
AKC

Almond shaped, moderately spaced and set a trifle obliquely. Eyes may be brown or blue in color; one of each or parti-colored are acceptable. Faults: Eyes set too obliquely; set too close together.

Expression is keen, but friendly; interested and even mischievous.

The head is finely chiselled with a fox-like appearance.

The eyes are set obliquely; forward-facing eyes would be exposed to driving snow and ice.

KC

Almond-shaped, moderately spaced and set obliquely. Any shade of blue or brown, one of each colour, or parti-colours equally acceptable. Expression keen, but friendly, interested, even mischievous.

The Standards agree on the desirable expression for the Siberian, and this stems mainly from the shape and placement of the eyes and ears. The eyes are of almond shape and tilted up at the outside corners. This gives the dog a faintly oriental look, together with a mischievous alertness. Round-shaped or level-set eyes would give a softer but duller expression.

The KC Standard says the eyes should be set obliquely, whereas the AKC asks for them to be set "a trifle obliquely". Other sled dog breeds also have eyes set obliquely and this is related to the dog's function and its environment. Prominent or forward-facing eyes are more susceptible to injury from driving snow and ice. The almond shape and oblique set can squint and deflect such problems more efficiently. The Siberian is the only sled dog for whom blue eyes, and any shade of brown from yellow to almost black, are all equally acceptable.

EARS
AKC

Of medium size, triangular in shape, close fitting and set high on the head. They are thick, well furred, slightly arched at the back, and strongly erect, with slightly rounded tips pointing straight up. **Faults: Ears too large in proportion to the head; too wide set; not strongly erect.**

KC

Medium size, relatively close together, triangular in shape, the height slightly greater than width at base. Set high on head, strongly erect, the inner edges being quite close together at the base, when the dog is at attention carried practically parallel. Slightly arched at the back. Thick, well furred outside and inside, tips slightly rounded.

The ears of a Siberian are set high on the head and are strongly erect. This contributes to the expression of alertness and interest. The KC Standard mentions that when the dog is at attention, the ears are practically parallel. All the sled dog breeds have erect, triangular, well-furred ears, but differ in exact shape and placement on the head. The Siberian is unique in the ears being set atop the head rather than somewhat to the side. This does not reduce the mobility of the ears, as the Siberian can easily rotate and/or flatten them depending on his mood, what he wishes to convey to another dog, or whether he is listening to something ahead, beside or behind. They can be pointing one ear forwards at another dog in a display of dominance while pointing the other backwards at you as you remonstrate!

MOUTH
AKC
Lips: Well pigmented and close fitting. Teeth: Closing in a scissors bite. Fault: Any bite other than scissors.

KC
Lips well pigmented, close fitting. Jaws strong, with a perfect, regular and complete scissor bite, i.e. upper teeth closely overlapping lower teeth and set square to the jaws.

Both Standards require close-fitting, well-pigmented lips. The latter is important because snow and ice can collect in the corners of a slack mouth and cause injury. Snow reflects ultra-violet light, which can cause skin cancer on exposed non-pigmented areas.

The scissor bite is the most natural dental conformation. It allows the dog to perform all the functions required of his front teeth, including nipping morsels from a bone, and grooming himself. In the UK a level bite is tolerated because it also allows all these functions, but it is not encouraged, as the upper and lower incisors will gradually wear each other away.

Ears are medium-sized and set high on the head.

NECK
AKC
Medium in length, arched and carried proudly erect when dog is standing. When moving at a trot, the neck is extended so that the head is carried slightly forward. Faults: Neck too short and thick; neck too long.

KC
Medium length and thickness, arched and carried proudly erect when standing. When moving at a trot, extended so that the head is carried slightly forward.

This is described as being medium in length. That is, it must be in proportion to the size of the dog. A rule of thumb, which can be used here, is that a medium length neck will be roughly the same length from occiput to withers as the dog's head is from tip of nose to occiput. It is normal for the neck to be thickly furred with hair longer than that on the head, sometimes forming an attractive ruff that frames the face. This can make the neck appear to be shorter than it really is.

A short neck is undesirable, as it is normally accompanied by short bones throughout the body, impinging on the dog's ability to work in harness. Similarly, an over-long neck not only looks odd, but also unbalances the dog, again with consequences to his fitness for function.

FOREQUARTERS
AKC
Chest: Deep and strong, but not too broad, with the deepest point being just behind and level with the elbows. The ribs are well sprung from the spine but flattened on the sides to allow for freedom of action. Faults: Chest too broad; "barrel ribs"; ribs too flat or weak. Shoulder: The shoulder blade is well laid back. The upper arm angles slightly backward from point of shoulder to elbow, and is never perpendicular to the ground. The muscles and ligaments holding the shoulder to the rib cage are firm and well developed. Faults: Straight

shoulders; loose shoulders. **Forelegs: When standing and viewed from the front, the legs are moderately spaced, parallel and straight, with the elbows close to the body and turned neither in nor out. Viewed from the side, pasterns are slightly slanted, with the pastern joint strong, but flexible. Bone is substantial but never heavy. Length of the leg from elbow to ground is slightly more than the distance from the elbow to the top of withers. Dewclaws on forelegs may be removed. Faults: Weak pasterns; too heavy bone; too narrow or too wide in the front; out at the elbows.**

KC

Shoulder blade well laid back, upper arm angles slightly backward from point of shoulder to elbow, never perpendicular to the ground. Muscle holding shoulder to rib cage firm and well-developed. Straight or loose shoulders highly undesirable. Viewed from the front, forelegs moderately spaced, parallel and straight with elbows close to the body, turning neither in nor out. Viewed from the side, pasterns slightly sloping, wrist strong but flexible. Length from elbow to ground slightly more than distance from elbows to top of withers. Bone proportionate, never heavy. Dewclaws may be removed.

Judges and breeders must remember that the Siberian Husky's function in life is to pull a light load (two to three times its own body weight) at moderate speed (12-16 miles per hour/19-26 kms per hour) for long distances (over 20 miles/32 km per day and up to 80 miles/128 km in some instances). Higher speeds can be achieved over shorter distances. Other sled-dog breeds pull heavier loads at lower speeds. Non-sledding breeds generally have only their own body weight to move around. In order to perform this work well, and without undue wear and tear on his body, a Siberian Husky must have correct conformation for the breed, as any lack will surely have a detrimental effect upon performance and working longevity.

The shoulder and foreleg bears the brunt of impact when the husky is loping and galloping. The Standards therefore require that the shoulder and upper arm is set at a sufficient angle to each other and to the spine, that, on impact, they can fold or give somewhat, absorbing the shock. The angles also allow for the shoulder blade and upper arm bones to be longer than they would be if this part of the leg were straighter. This gives the dog a longer stride, and more bone surface area for muscle attachments. The pastern also slopes at a moderate angle, assisting in shock absorption.

BODY
AKC

The back is straight and strong, with a level topline from withers to croup. It is of medium length, neither cobby nor slack from excessive length. The loin is taut and lean, narrower than the rib cage, and with a slight tuck-up.

The back is straight and strong.

The croup slopes away from the spine at an angle, but never so steeply as to restrict the rearward thrust of the hind legs. Faults: Weak or slack back; roached back; sloping topline.

KC

Straight and strong, with level topline from withers to croup. Medium length, not cobby, nor slack from excessive length. In profile, body from point of shoulder to rear point of croup slightly longer than height from ground to top of withers. Chest deep and strong but not too broad, deepest point being just behind and level with elbows. Ribs well sprung from spine but flattened on sides to allow for freedom of action. Loins slightly arched, well muscled, taut and lean, narrower than rib cage with a slight tuck-up. Croup slopes away from spine at an angle, but never so steeply as to restrict the rearward thrust of hind legs.

A dog that is going to pull a load all day at a lope or trot must have a good 'engine'. Lungs provide the muscles with oxygen and excrete the waste carbon dioxide. The heart must have sufficient room in the chest to beat efficiently. This requires the Siberian Husky to have a ribcage that combines maximum internal space with a shape that is conducive to function as a set of bellows. Therefore, the Siberian has a ribcage that is long and deep (to maximise room for the lungs and heart), but not too broad, as this

reduces the effectiveness of the bellows action. The ribcage is also slightly flattened at the sides to allow the upper forelimbs to glide across it smoothly. Siberians can take up to three years to fully develop in body and coat, so frequently appear to be rather slight and shallow-chested until they mature.

Very little flexion occurs in the part of the spine that supports the ribcage. The necessary flexibility needed for loping and galloping comes from the lumbar spine in the loin area. It follows that the loin needs to be firmly muscled and taut to support the spine, while being long enough to be flexible; too long and the loin becomes slack and weak, too

The hind legs are the powerhouse, and should be well-muscled and strong to propel the dog forward.

short and it becomes too stiff to flex adequately.

A Siberian should always look from above as if it has a definite waist, before broadening somewhat at the pelvis.

The area of the back from the pin bones to the root of the tail is called the croup. This should slope downwards towards the tail at an angle of approximately 30 degrees from the horizontal. This is the angle that allows the most flexion of the loin with the greatest thrust from the hind legs. The croup angle reflects the set of the pelvis on to the spine and therefore has a direct bearing on the action of the hind legs. If the angle is too steep, the dog will have insufficient thrust to propel itself efficiently. If the croup is too flat, the dog will lack length of stride.

The length of the croup is also important as the pelvis provides attachment for the major locomotion muscles of the hindquarters. A short croup means that attachment area is restricted and therefore there will be less muscle to drive the dog.

HINDQUARTERS
AKC

When standing and viewed from the rear, the hind legs are moderately spaced and parallel. The upper thighs are well muscled and powerful, the stifles well bent, the hock joint well-defined and set low to the ground. Dewclaws, if any, are to be removed. Faults: Straight stifles, cow-hocks, too narrow or too wide in the rear.

KC

Viewed from rear, hind legs moderately spaced and parallel. Upper thighs well muscled and powerful, stifles well bent, hock joint well defined and set low to ground.

The rear legs propel the husky and his load forward. To do this efficiently, the big muscles that flex and extend the legs must have the correct underlying bone structure to produce good leverage. The rear angles and bone lengths of the pelvis and femur (thigh bone) should reflect those of the forequarters. The stifle, or knee, of a Siberian Husky should be a little nearer to the body than that of heavy freighting sled dogs, with a somewhat longer second thigh. This is in keeping with the structure of a dog built for running rather than trotting.

FEET

AKC

Oval in shape but not long. The paws are medium in size, compact and well furred between the toes and pads. The pads are tough and thickly cushioned. The paws neither turn in nor out when the dog is in natural stance. Faults: Soft or splayed toes; paws too large and clumsy; paws too small and delicate; toeing in or out.

KC

Oval, not long, turning neither in nor out in natural stance. Medium size, compact, well furred and slightly webbed between toes. Pads tough and

thickly cushioned. Trimming of fur between toes and around feet permissible.

The paws are adapted for running on snow. They are oval in shape, well furred with tight toes. This reduces the accumulation of ice and snow between the pads, which could otherwise make the husky lame.

TAIL

AKC

The well furred tail of fox-brush shape is set on just below the level of the topline, and is usually carried over the back in a graceful sickle curve when the dog is at attention. When carried up, the tail does not curl to either side of the body, nor does it snap flat against the back. A

Tail carriage when the dog is animated.

The judge will ask you to run a triangle on a loose lead so the dog's movement can be assessed from the front, side and rear.

When trotting, the Siberian Husky should single track, with his paws falling in a single line beneath the centre of his body.

trailing tail is normal for the dog when in repose. Hair on the tail is of medium length and approximately the same length on top, sides and bottom, giving the appearance of a round brush. Faults: A snapped or tightly curled tail; highly plumed tail; tail set too low or too high.

KC
Well furred, or round, fox brush shape set on just below level of topline and usually carried over back in graceful sickle curve when dog at attention. When carried up, tail should not curl too tightly, nor should it curl to either side of body, or snap flat against back. Hair on tail of medium length and approximately same length all

round. A trailing tail is normal for the dog when working or in repose.

Both Standards agree on the set of the tail, i.e. the position of the base of the tail where it joins the dog's body. It should be a little below the level of the back if the croup is sufficiently sloped. It does not form a full curl but a gentle open curve above the back when the husky is alert. The desired length of tail is not mentioned, and the tails of Siberian Huskies do vary in length. However, there is an expectation that the tail will not look so short, nor so long, as to be out of proportion with the rest of the dog.

The tail is described as fox-brush in shape. That is, it is fully furred all the way round and finishing at

something of a point at the tip, which is often, but not always, white. If you remember that Siberian Huskies are adapted to sleep outside in temperatures down to minus 40 degrees Centigrade, it is obvious that complete coverage of good, dense fur is essential to avoid freezing of extremities, such as the tail.

GAIT/MOVEMENT
AKC
The Siberian Husky's characteristic gait is smooth and seemingly effortless. He is quick and light on his feet, and when in the show ring should be gaited on a loose lead at a moderately fast trot, exhibiting good reach in the forequarters and good drive in the hindquarters. When viewed

from the front to rear while moving at a walk the Siberian Husky does not single-track, but as the speed increases the legs gradually angle inward until the pads are falling on a line directly under the longitudinal center of the body. As the pad marks converge, the forelegs and hind legs are carried straightforward, with neither elbows nor stifles turned in or out. Each hind leg moves in the path of the foreleg on the same side. While the dog is gaiting, the topline remains firm and level. *Faults:* Short, prancing or choppy gait, lumbering or rolling gait; crossing or crabbing.

KC

Smooth and seemingly effortless. Quick and light on feet, gaited on a loose lead at a moderately fast trot, exhibiting good reach in forequarters and good drive in hindquarters. When walking, legs move in parallel, but as speed increases, gradually angling inward to single track. As pad marks converge, forelegs and hind legs carried straight with neither elbows nor stifles turning in nor out, each hind leg moving in path of foreleg on same side. Topline of back remaining firm and level during gaiting.

The Siberian Husky is a long-distance athlete. He is built to lope or gallop while pulling a load. Trotting around a show ring or going for a walk with you should be no effort to him. In fact, a well-made Siberian can look almost indolent as he floats around a show ring, showing no sign of effort or exertion at all. It follows that a Siberian who trots in a busy or flashy manner is likely to be structurally incorrect for the breed.

COAT
AKC

The coat of the Siberian Husky is double and medium in length, giving a well furred appearance, but is never so long as to obscure the clean-cut outline of the dog. The undercoat is soft and dense and of sufficient length to support the outer coat. The guard hairs of the outer coat are straight and somewhat smooth lying, never harsh nor standing straight off from the body. It should be noted that the absence of the undercoat during the shedding season is normal. Trimming of whiskers and fur between the toes and around the feet to present a neater appearance is permissible. Trimming the fur on any other part of the dog is not to be condoned and should be severely penalized. Faults: Long, rough, or shaggy coat; texture too harsh or too silky; trimming of the coat, except as permitted above.

KC

Double, and medium in length, giving a well furred appearance, never so long as to obscure clean-cut outline of dog. Undercoat soft and dense; of sufficient length to support outer coat. Guard hairs of outer coat straight and somewhat smooth-lying, never harsh, rough or shaggy, too silky nor standing straight off from body. Absence of undercoat during shedding normal. No trimming of fur on any part of dog, except feet.

The coat of a Siberian is more akin to fur than to the hair of most dogs. The undercoat is dense and soft and, when parted, you can barely see any skin. The top coat is longer and straight, and does not stand off from the dog's body except that part that frames the head. It should feel neither harsh nor silky.

In summer the Siberian husky will grow a shorter, thinner coat after moulting heavily, swapping this back for his winter coat in the autumn. He is adapted to sleep outside in cold dry conditions. This is why his coat should not be too long or fluffy, since such a coat allows the formation of ice.

Bathing is seldom necessary, as dirt simply falls away from the correct coat. No coat trimming is allowed except to tidy the feet. Trimming elsewhere should be heavily penalised by judges, as it is an attempt to deceive as to the dog's suitability for his native environment.

COLOUR
AKC

All colors from black to pure white are allowed. A variety of

Any colour is acceptable in the Breed Standard, none is more or less desirable in the show ring, and no colour is more rare than any other.

markings on the head is common, including many striking patterns not found in other breeds.

KC

All colours and markings, including white, allowed. Variety of markings on head is common, including many striking patterns not found in other breeds.

All colours are allowed. However, the most common colour is various shades of grey, followed by black, red and white. The undercoat is not necessarily the same colour or shade as the top coat. The shade can also vary somewhat between the summer and winter coats.

There are many beautiful coat markings in this breed, particularly on the head and chest. Piebalds of various colours are as acceptable as solid colours. There is no such thing as a mismark.

SIZE
AKC
Height: **Dogs, 21 to 23.5 inches at the withers. Bitches, 20 to 22** inches at the withers. *Weight*: **Dogs, 45 to 60 pounds. Bitches, 35 to 50 pounds. Weight is in proportion to height. The measurements mentioned above represent the extreme height and weight limits with no preference given to either extreme. Any appearance of excessive bone or weight should be penalized. In profile, the length of the body from the point of the shoulder to the rear point of the croup is slightly longer than the height of the body from the ground to the top of the withers. Disqualification:**

Dogs over 23.5 inches and bitches over 22 inches.

KC
Height: dogs: 53-60 cm (21-23.5 in) at withers; bitches: 51-56 cm (20-22 in) at withers. Weight: dogs: 20-27 kg (45-60 lb); bitches: 16-23 kg (35-50 lb). Weight should be in proportion to height. These measurements represent the extremes in height and weight, with no preference given to either extreme. A dog should not exceed 60 cm (23.5 in) or a bitch exceed 56 cm (22 in).

The striking difference between the AKC Standard and that of the KC is the position taken on the subject of height. In the AKC Standard, dogs and bitches that exceed the maximum heights stipulated are disqualified. Those who fail to reach the minimum are not mentioned. In the UK, height is just one factor in assessing the quality of the dog, and some leeway in either direction is permissible.

SUMMARY
AKC
The most important breed characteristics of the Siberian Husky are medium size, moderate bone, well balanced proportions, ease and freedom of movement, proper coat, pleasing head and ears, correct tail, and good disposition. Any appearance of excessive bone or weight, constricted or clumsy gait, or long, rough coat should be penalized. The Siberian Husky never appears so heavy or coarse as to suggest a freighting animal; nor is he so light and fragile as to suggest a sprint-racing animal. In both sexes the Siberian Husky gives the appearance of being capable of great endurance. In addition to the faults already noted, the obvious structural faults common to all breeds are as undesirable in the Siberian Husky as in any other breed, even though they are not specifically mentioned herein.

KC
Not included.

FAULTS
AKC
Listed under headings.

KC
Faults: Any departure from the foregoing points should be considered a fault and the seriousness with which the fault should be regarded should be in exact proportion to its degree and its effect upon the health and welfare of the dog.
Note: Male animals should have two apparently normal testicles fully descended.

Although the KC stipulates that males should have two apparently normal testicles, neutered males can be shown on equal terms, provided veterinary evidence is available to confirm his 'normality' in this department prior to surgery.

DISQUALIFICATION
AKC
Dogs over 23.5 inches and bitches over 22 inches.

KC
Not included.

SUMMING UP
It would be a great shame if the dog developed over hundreds of years by the Chukchi tribe in Siberia were to be lost to future generations.

Unfortunately, the Soviets tried to destroy the native dog breeds of the Siberian tribes as a way to subjugate these peoples. Luckily, some Siberian Huskies had been taken to Alaska and their merits as supreme racing sled dogs were recognised and valued enough to be preserved.

It behoves those of us who have custody of the descendants of these exported dogs to respect their origins and keep them as close to their original form as we can manage. Changing them into something more convenient for our current lifestyles would effectively finish what the Soviets started.

As with so many old breeds of various domestic species, we can never be sure that we will not need them again, so let us preserve and enjoy them.

HAPPY AND HEALTHY

Chapter

The Siberian Husky is renowned as a faithful companion and a willing friend on a non-conditional basis, whose life span often runs into double figures. He will, however, of necessity rely on you for food and shelter, accident prevention and medication. A healthy Siberian Husky is a happy chap, looking to please and amuse his owner.

Some genetic conditions have been recognised in the Siberian Husky, which will be covered in depth later in the chapter.

VACCINATION

There is much debate over the issue of vaccination at the moment. The timing of the final part of the initial vaccination course for a puppy and the frequency of subsequent booster vaccinations are both under scrutiny. An evaluation of the relative risk for each disease plays a part, depending on the local situation.

Many owners think that the actual vaccination is the protection, so that their puppy can go out for walks as soon as he or she has had the final part of the puppy vaccination course. This is not the case. The rationale behind vaccination is to stimulate the immune system into producing protective antibodies, which will be triggered if the patient is subsequently exposed to that particular disease. This means that a further one or two weeks will have to pass before an effective level of protection will have developed.

Vaccines against viruses stimulate longer-lasting protection than those against bacteria, whose effect may only persist for a matter of months in some cases.

There is also the possibility of an individual failing to mount a full immune response to a vaccination: although the vaccine schedule may have been followed as recommended, that particular dog remains vulnerable.

A dog's level of protection against rabies, as demonstrated by the antibody titre in a blood sample, used to be routinely tested in the UK in order to fulfil the requirements of the Pet Travel Scheme (PETS). However, since 1st January 2012, this only applies in certain circumstances (see page 131). This is not required at the current time with any other individual diseases in order to gauge the need for booster vaccination or to determine the effect of a course of vaccines; instead, your veterinary surgeon will advise a protocol based upon the vaccines available, local disease prevalence, and the lifestyle of you and your dog.

It is worth remembering that maintaining a fully effective level of immune protection against the disease appropriate to your locale is vital: these are serious diseases, which may result in the death of your dog, and some may have the potential to be passed on to his human family (so-called zoonotic potential for transmission). This is where you will be grateful for your veterinary surgeon's own knowledge and advice.

The American Animal Hospital Association laid down guidance at the end of 2006 for the vaccination of dogs in North America. Core diseases were defined as distemper, adenovirus, parvovirus and rabies. So-called non-core diseases are kennel cough, Lyme disease and leptospirosis. A decision to vaccinate against one or more non-core diseases will be based on an individual's level of risk, determined on lifestyle and where you live in the US.

Do remember, however, that the booster visit to the veterinary surgery is not 'just' for a booster. I am regularly correcting my clients when they announce that they have 'just' brought their pet for a booster. Instead, this appointment is a chance for a full health check and evaluation of how a particular dog is doing. After all, we are all conversant with the adage that a human year is equivalent to seven canine years.

There have been attempts in recent times to reset the scale for two reasons: small breeds live longer than giant breeds, and dogs are living longer than previously. I have seen dogs of 17 and 18 years of age, but to say a dog is 119 or 126 years old is plainly meaningless. It does emphasise the fact, though, that a dog's health can change dramatically over the course of a single year, because dogs age at a far faster rate than humans.

For me as a veterinary surgeon, the booster vaccination visit is a challenge: how much can I find of which the owner was unaware, such as rotten teeth or a heart murmur? Even monitoring bodyweight year upon year is of use, because bodyweight can creep up, or down, without an owner realising. Being overweight is unhealthy, but it may take an outsider's remark to make an owner realise that there is a problem. Conversely, a drop in bodyweight may be the only pointer to an underlying problem.

The diseases against which dogs are vaccinated include:

ADENOVIRUS

Canine adenovirus 1 (CAV-1) affects the liver (hepatitis) and is seen within affected dogs as the classic 'blue eye', while CAV-2 is a cause of kennel cough (see later). Vaccines often include both canine adenoviruses.

DISTEMPER

This disease is sometimes called 'hardpad' from the characteristic changes to the pads of the paws. It has a worldwide distribution, but fortunately vaccination has been very effective at reducing its occurrence. It is caused by a virus and affects the respiratory, gastro-intestinal (gut) and nervous

All plants look tasty to puppies – even those which may be harmful.

LEPTOSPIROSIS

This disease is caused by *Leptospira interrogans*, a spiral-shaped bacterium. There are several natural variants or serovars. Each is characteristically found in one or more particular host animal species, which then acts as a reservoir, intermittently shedding leptospires in the urine. Infection can also be picked up at mating, via bite wounds, across the placenta, or through eating the carcases of infected animals (such as rats).

A serovar will cause actual clinical disease in an individual when two conditions are fulfilled: the individual is not the natural host species, and is also not immune to that particular serovar.

Leptospirosis is a zoonotic disease, known as Weil's disease in humans, with implications for all those in contact with an affected dog. It is also commonly called rat jaundice, reflecting the rat's important role as a carrier. The UK National Rodent Survey 2003 found a wild brown rat population of 60 million, equivalent at the time to one rat per person. Wherever you live in the UK, rats are endemic, which means that there is as much a risk to the Siberian Husky living with a family in a town as the Siberian Husky leading a rural lifestyle.

Signs of illness reflect the organs affected by a particular serovar. In humans, there may be a flu-like illness or a more serious, often life-threatening disorder involving major body organs. The illness in a susceptible dog may be mild, the dog recovering within two to three weeks without treatment but going on to develop long-term liver or kidney disease. In contrast, peracute illness may result in a rapid deterioration and death following an initial malaise and fever. There may also be anorexia, vomiting, diarrhoea, abdominal pain, joint pain, increased thirst and urination rate, jaundice, and ocular changes. Haemorrhage is also a common feature, manifesting as bleeding under the skin, nosebleeds, and the presence of blood in the urine and faeces.

Treatment requires rigorous intravenous fluid therapy to support the kidneys. Being a bacterial infection, it is possible to treat leptospirosis with specific antibiotics, although a prolonged course of several weeks is needed. Strict hygiene and barrier nursing are required in order to avoid onward transmission of the disease.

Annual vaccination is recommended for leptospirosis because the immunity only lasts for a year, unlike the longer immunity associated with vaccines against viruses. There is, however, little or no cross-protection between Leptospira serovars, so vaccination will result in protection against only those serovars included in the particular vaccine used. Additionally, although vaccination against leptospirosis will prevent active disease if an individual is exposed to a serovar included in the vaccine, it cannot prevent infection of that individual and the dog becoming a carrier in the long-term. In the UK, vaccines have classically included *L. icterohaemorrhagiae* (rat-adapted serovar) and *L. canicola* (dog-specific serovar). The latter is of especial significance to us humans, since disease will not be apparent in an infected dog but leptospires will be shed intermittently.

Kennel Cough can spread rapidly among dogs that live together.

systems, so it causes a wide range of illnesses. Fox and urban stray dog populations are most at risk and are usually responsible for local outbreaks.

KENNEL COUGH

Also known as infectious tracheobronchitis, *Bordetella bronchiseptica* is not only a major cause of kennel cough but also a common secondary infection on top of another cause. Being a bacterium, it is susceptible to treatment with appropriate antibiotics, but the immunity stimulated by the vaccine is therefore short-lived (six to 12 months).

This vaccine is often in a form to be administered down the nostrils in order to stimulate local immunity at the point of entry, so to speak. Do not be alarmed to see your veterinary surgeon using a needle and syringe to draw up the vaccine, because the needle will be replaced with a special

plastic introducer, allowing the vaccine to be gently instilled into each nostril. Dogs generally resent being held more than the actual intra-nasal vaccine, and I have learnt that covering the patient's eyes helps greatly.

Kennel cough is, however, rather a catch-all term for any cough spreading within a dog population – not just in kennels, but also between dogs at a training session or breed show, or even mixing in the park. Many of these infections may not be *B. bronchiseptica* but other viruses, for which one can only treat symptomatically. Parainfluenza virus is often included in a vaccine programme, as it is a common viral cause of kennel cough.

Kennel cough can seem alarming. There is a persistent cough accompanied by the production of white frothy spittle, which can last for a matter of weeks; during this time the

patient is highly infectious to other dogs. I remember when it ran through our five Border Collies – there were white patches of froth on the floor wherever you looked! Other features include sneezing, a runny nose, and eyes sore with conjunctivitis. Fortunately, these infections are generally self-limiting, most dogs recovering without any long-lasting problems, but an elderly dog may be knocked sideways by it, akin to the effects of a common cold on a frail, elderly person.

LYME DISEASE

This is a bacterial infection transmitted by hard ticks. It is restricted to those specific areas of the US where ticks are found, such as the north-eastern states, some southern states, California and the upper Mississippi region. It does also occur in the UK, but at a low level, so vaccination is not routinely offered.

Clinical disease is manifested primarily as limping due to arthritis, but other organs affected include the heart, kidneys and nervous system. It is readily treatable with appropriate antibiotics, once diagnosed, but the causal bacterium, *Borrelia burgdorferi*, is not cleared from the body totally and will persist.

Prevention requires both vaccination and tick control, especially as there are other diseases transmitted by ticks. Ticks carrying *B. burgdorferi* will transmit it to humans as well, but an infected dog cannot pass it to a human.

Find out whether Lyme disease occurs in your area. At the present time, it is relatively rare in the UK.

PARVOVIRUS (CPV)

Canine parvovirus disease first appeared in the late 1970s, when it was feared that the UK's dog population would be decimated by it because of the lack of immunity in the general canine population. While this was a terrifying possibility at the time, fortunately it did not happen.

There are two forms of the virus (CPV-1, CPV-2) affecting domesticated dogs. It is highly contagious, picked up via the mouth/nose from infected faeces. The incubation period is about five days. CPV-2 causes two types of illness: gastro-enteritis and heart disease in puppies born to unvaccinated dams, both of which often result in death. Infection of puppies under three weeks of age with CPV-1

manifests as diarrhoea, vomiting, difficulty breathing, and fading puppy syndrome. CPV-1 can cause abortion and foetal abnormalities in breeding bitches.

Occurrence is mainly low now, thanks to vaccination, although a recent outbreak in my area did claim the lives of several dogs. It is also occasionally seen in the elderly unvaccinated dog.

RABIES

This is another zoonotic disease and there are very strict control measures in place. Vaccines were once available in the UK only on an individual basis for dogs being taken abroad. Pets travelling into the UK had to serve six months' compulsory quarantine so that any pet incubating rabies would be identified before release back

into the general population. Under the UK Pet Travel Scheme (PETS), provided certain criteria are met (check the DEFRA website for up-to-date information – www.defra.gov.uk) then dogs can enter the UK without being quarantined. In essence, a dog living in EU and specified non-EU countries such as the USA can travel twenty-one days after being microchipped and vaccinated against rabies. The requirement for a blood test thirty days after rabies vaccination, with a result demonstrating effective immunity, still applies to dogs from certain non-EU countries such as South Africa, together with a three month wait from the date of that blood test before being allowed to enter the UK.

You will need to continue the worming programme started by your puppy's breeder.

PARASITES

A parasite is defined as an organism deriving benefit on a one-way basis from another, the host. It goes without saying that it is not to the parasite's advantage to harm the host to such an extent that the benefit is lost, especially if it results in the death of the host. This means a dog could harbour parasites, internal and/or external, without there being any signs apparent to the owner. Many canine parasites can, however, transfer to humans with variable consequences, so routine preventative treatment is advised against particular parasites.

Just as with vaccination, risk assessment plays a part – for example, there is no need for routine heartworm treatment in the UK (at present), but it is vital in the US and in Mediterranean countries.

ROUNDWORMS (NEMATODES)

These are the spaghetti-like worms that you may have seen passed in faeces or brought up in vomit. Most of the deworming treatments in use today cause the adult roundworms to disintegrate, thankfully, so that treating puppies in particular is not as unpleasant as it used to be!

Most puppies will have a worm burden, mainly of a particular roundworm species (*Toxocara canis*), which reactivates within the dam's tissues during pregnancy and passes to the foetuses developing in the womb. It is therefore important to treat the dam both during and after pregnancy, as well as the puppies.

Dogs to be imported into the US have to show that they were vaccinated against rabies at least 30 days previously; otherwise, they have to serve effective internal quarantine for 30 days from the date of vaccination against rabies, in order to ensure they are not incubating rabies. The exception is dogs entering from countries recognised as being rabies-free, in which case it has to be proved that they lived in that country for at least six months beforehand. Regulations do change, so ensure you have up-to-date information.

TAPEWORMS (CESTODES)

When considering the general dog population, the primary source of the commonest tapeworm species will be fleas, which can carry the eggs. Most multi-wormers will be active against these tapeworms. They are not a threat to human health, but it is unpleasant to see the wriggly ricegrain tapeworm segments emerging from your dog's back passage while he is lying in front of the fire, and usually when you have guests for dinner!

A tapeworm of significance to human health is *Echinococcus granulosus*, found in a few parts of the UK, mainly in Wales. Man is an intermediate host for this tapeworm, along with sheep, cattle and pigs. Inadvertent ingestion of eggs passed in the faeces of an infected dog is followed by the development of so-called hydatid cysts in major organs, such as the lungs and liver, necessitating surgical removal. Dogs become infected through eating raw meat containing hydatid cysts. Cooking will kill hydatid cysts, so avoid feeding raw meat and offal in areas of high risk.

The specific requirements for treatment with praziquantel within 24 to 48 hours of entry into the UK under the Pet Travel Scheme are under review. They were put in place to prevent the inadvertent introduction of *Echinococcus multilocularis*, a tapeworm carried by foxes on mainland Europe, which is transmissible to humans, causing serious or even fatal liver disease. You should therefore still consider precautionary treatment of your dog.

Professional advice is to continue worming every one to three months. There are roundworm eggs in the environment and, unless you examine your dog's faeces under a microscope on a very regular basis for the presence of roundworm eggs, you will be unaware of your dog having picked up roundworms, unless he should have such a heavy burden that he passes the adults.

It takes a few weeks from the time that a dog swallows a *Toxocara canis* roundworm egg to himself passing viable eggs (the pre-patent period). These eggs are not immediately infective to other animals, requiring a period of maturation in the environment, which is primarily temperature-dependent and therefore shorter in the summer (as little as two weeks) than in the winter. The eggs can survive in the environment for two years and more.

There are deworming products that are active all the time, which will provide continuous protection when administered as often as directed. Otherwise, treating every month will, in effect, cut in before a dog could theoretically become a source of roundworm eggs to the general population.

It is the risk to human health that is so important: *T. canis* roundworms will migrate within our tissues and cause all manner of problems, not least of which (but fortunately rarely) is blindness. If a dog has roundworms, the eggs also find their way on to his coat where they can be picked up during stroking. Sensible hygiene is therefore important. You should always carefully pick up your dog's faeces and dispose of them appropriately, thereby preventing the maturation of any eggs present in the fresh faeces.

HEARTWORM

Heartworm infection has been diagnosed in dogs all over the world. There are two prerequisites: the presence of mosquitoes, and a warm, humid climate.

When a female mosquito bites an infected animal, it acquires *D. immitis* in its circulating form, as microfilariae. A warm environmental temperature is needed for these microfilariae to develop into the infective third-stage larvae (L3) within the mosquitoes, the so-called intermediate host. L3 larvae are then transmitted by the mosquito when it next bites a dog. Therefore, while heartworm infection is found in all parts of the United States, it is at differing levels. An occurrence in Alaska, for example, is probably a reflection of a visiting dog having previously picked up the infection elsewhere.

Heartworm infection is not currently a problem in the UK, except for those dogs contracting it while abroad without suitable preventative treatment. Global warming and its effect on the UK's climate, however, could change that.

It is a potentially life-threatening condition, with dogs of all breeds and ages being susceptible without preventative treatment. The larvae can grow to 14 inches within the right side of the heart, causing primarily signs of heart failure and ultimately liver and kidney damage. It can be treated but prevention is a better plan. In the US, regular blood tests for the presence of infection are advised, coupled with appropriate preventative measures, so I would advise liaison with your veterinary surgeon.

For dogs travelling to heartworm-endemic areas of the EU, such as the Mediterranean coast, preventative treatment should be started before leaving the UK and maintained during the visit. Again, this is best arranged with your veterinary surgeon.

FLEAS

There are several species of flea, which are not host-specific. A dog can be carrying cat and human fleas as well as dog fleas, but the same flea treatment will kill and/or control them all. It is also accepted that environmental control is a vital part of a flea control programme. This is because the adult flea is only on the animal for as long as it takes to have a blood meal and to breed; the remainder of the life cycle occurs in the house, car, caravan, shed…

There is a vast array of flea control products available, with various routes of administration: collar, powder, spray, 'spot-on', or oral. Flea control needs to be applied to all pets in the house, regardless of whether they leave the house, since fleas can be introduced into the home by other pets and their human owners. Discuss your specific flea control needs with your veterinary surgeon.

LUNGWORM

Lungworm, or *Angiostrongylus vasorum*, is a parasite that lives in the heart and major blood vessels supplying the lungs. It can cause many problems, including, ultimately, death. The parasite is carried by slugs and snails, and the dog becomes infected when ingesting these, often accidentally when rummaging through undergrowth. Lungworm is not common, but it is on the increase and a responsible owner should be

Discuss flea control with your vet.

aware of it. Fortunately, it is easily preventable and even affected dogs usually make a full recovery if treated early enough. Your vet will be able to advise you on the risks in your area and what form of treatment may be required.

MITES

There are five types of mite that can affect dogs.

Demodex canis: This mite is a normal inhabitant of canine hair follicles, passed from the bitch to her pups as they suckle. The development of actual skin disease or demodicosis depends on the individual. It is seen frequently around the time of puberty and after a bitch's first season, associated with hormonal changes. There may, however, be an inherited weakness in an individual's immune system, enabling multiplication of the mite.

The localised form consists of areas of fur loss without itchiness, generally around the face and on the forelimbs, and 90 per cent will recover without treatment. The other 10 per cent develop the juvenile-onset generalised form, of which half will recover spontaneously. The other half may be depressed, go off their food, and show signs of itchiness due to secondary bacterial skin infections.

Treatment is often prolonged over several months and consists of regular bathing with a specific miticidal shampoo, often clipping away fur to improve access to the skin, together with a suitable antibiotic by mouth. There is also now a licensed 'spot-on' preparation available. Progress is monitored by the examination of deep skin scrapings for the presence of the mite; the initial diagnosis is based upon abnormally high numbers of the

mite, often with live individuals being seen.

Some Siberian Huskies may develop demodicosis for the first time in middle-age (more than four years of age). This often reflects underlying immunosuppression by an internal disease, so it is important to identify such a cause and correct it where possible, as well as treating the skin condition.

Sarcoptes scabei: This characteristically causes an intense pruritus or itchiness in the affected Siberian Husky, causing him to incessantly scratch and bite at himself, leading to marked fur loss and skin trauma. Initially starting on the elbows, earflaps and hocks, without treatment the skin on the rest of the body can become affected, with thickening and pigmentation of the skin. Secondary bacterial infections are common.

Unlike Demodex, this mite lives at the skin surface, and it can be hard to find in skin scrapings. It is therefore not unusual to treat a patient for sarcoptic mange (scabies) based on the appearance of the problem even with negative skin scrapings, and especially if there is a history of contact with foxes, which are a frequent source of the scabies mite.

It will spread between dogs and can therefore also be found in situations where large numbers of dogs are mixing together. It will cause itchiness in humans, although the mite cannot complete its life cycle on us, so treating all affected dogs should be sufficient. Fortunately, there are now highly effective 'spot-on' treatments for Sarcoptes scabei.

Cheyletiella yasguri: This is the fur mite most commonly found on dogs. It is often called 'walking dandruff' because it can be possible to see collections of the small white mite moving about over the skin surface. There is excessive scale, dandruff, and mild itchiness. It is transmissible to humans, causing a pruritic rash.

Diagnosis is by microscopic examination of skin scrapings, coat combings and sticky tape impressions from the skin and fur. Treatment is with an appropriate insecticide, as advised by your veterinary surgeon.

Otodectes cynotis: A highly transmissible otitis externa (outer ear infection) results from the presence in the outer ear canal of this ear mite, characterised by exuberant production of dark earwax. The patient will frequently shake his head and rub at the ear(s) affected. The mites can also spread on to the skin adjacent to the opening of the external ear canal, and may transfer elsewhere, such as to the paws.

TICKS

Ticks have become an increasing problem in recent years throughout Britain. Their physical presence causes irritation, but it is their potential to spread disease that causes concern. A tick will transmit any infection previously contracted while feeding on an animal: for example Borrelia burgdorferi, the causal agent of Lyme disease (see page 132).

The life cycle of the tick is curious: each life stage takes a year to develop and move on to the next. Long grass is a major habitat. The vibration of animals moving through the grass will stimulate the larva, nymph or adult to climb up a blade of grass and wave its legs in the air as it 'quests' for a host on to which to latch for its next blood meal. Humans are as likely to be hosts, so ramblers and orienteers are advised to cover their legs when going through rough long grass.

There are effective treatments against ticks. Removing a tick is simple – provided your dog will stay still. The important rule is to grip the tick as close to the dog's skin as possible and pull firmly but gently so that the tick is persuaded to let go with its mouthparts. Grasp the tick either between thumb and fingers, or with a specific tick-removing instrument, and then pull until the tick comes away. I keep a plastic tick hook in my wallet at all times. Ticks elsewhere in the world are an important vector of diseases. There was a requirement under the UK Pet Travel Scheme for tick treatment within 24-48 hours of a dog entering the UK. From 1st January 2012, this is no longer the case. You should, however, take action to protect your dog from picking up ticks if travelling abroad in a high risk area.

When using an otoscope to examine the outer ear canal, the heat from the light source will often cause any ear mites present to start moving around. I often offer owners the chance to have a look, because it really is quite an extraordinary sight! It is also possible to identify the mite from earwax smeared on to a slide and examined under a microscope.

Cats are a common source of ear mites. It is not unusual to find ear mites during the routine examination of puppies and kittens. Treatment options include specific eardrops acting against both the mite and any secondary infections present in the auditory canal, and certain 'spot-on' formulations. It is vital to treat all dogs and cats in the household to prevent recycling of the mite between individuals.

(Neo-) *Trombicula autumnalis*:
The free-living harvest mite can cause an intense local irritation on the skin. Its larvae are picked up from undergrowth, so they are characteristically found as a bright orange patch on the web of skin between the digits of the paws. It feeds on skin cells before dropping off to complete its life cycle in the environment.

Its name is a little misleading, because it is not restricted to the autumn nor to harvest-time; I find it on the earflaps of cats from late June onwards, depending on the weather. It will also bite humans.

Treatment depends on identifying and avoiding hotspots for picking up harvest mites, if possible. Checking the skin,

The responsible owner should have a basic knowledge of the ailments that most commonly affect dogs.

especially the paws, after exercise and mechanically removing any mites found will reduce the chances of irritation, which can be treated symptomatically. Insecticides can also be applied – be guided by your veterinary surgeon.

A-Z OF COMMON AILMENTS

ANAL SACS (IMPACTED)
The anal sacs lie on either side of the anus at approximately four and eight o'clock, if compared with the face of a clock. They fill with a particularly pungent fluid, which is emptied on to the faeces as they move past the sacs to exit from the anus. Theories abound as to why these sacs should become impacted periodically and seemingly more so in some dogs than others.

The irritation of impacted anal sacs is often seen as 'scooting', when the backside is dragged along the ground. Some dogs will also gnaw at their back feet or over the rump.

Increasing the fibre content of the diet helps some dogs; in others, there is underlying skin disease. It may be a one-off occurrence for no apparent reason. Sometimes an infection can become established, requiring antibiotic therapy, which may need to be coupled with flushing out the infected sac under sedation or general anaesthesia. More rarely, a dog will present with an apparently acute-onset anal sac abscess, which is incredibly painful.

DIARRHOEA
Cause and treatment much as Gastritis (see below).

EAR INFECTIONS
The dog has a long external ear canal, initially vertical then horizontal, leading to the eardrum, which protects the

middle ear. If your Siberian Husky is shaking his head, then his ears will need to be inspected with an auroscope by a veterinary surgeon in order to identify any cause, and to ensure the eardrum is intact. A sample may be taken from the canal to be examined under the microscope and cultured, to identify causal agents before prescribing appropriate eardrops containing antibiotic, antifungal agent and/or steroid. Predisposing causes of otitis externa or infection in the external ear canal include:

- Presence of a foreign body, such as a grass awn/seed
- Ear mites, which are intensely irritating to the dog and stimulate the production of brown wax, predisposing to infection
- Previous infections, causing the canal's lining to thicken, narrowing the canal and reducing ventilation
- Bathing/swimming– water trapped in the external ear canal can lead to infection, especially if the water is not clean.

FOREIGN BODIES

- Internal: Non-digestible items can cause problems if they are swallowed and then lodge in the stomach or obstruct the intestines, necessitating surgical removal. Acute vomiting is the

Take care exercising your dog in long grass as grass awns entering the body can cause problems.

main indication. Common objects I have seen removed include garden stones, peach stones, babies' dummies, golf balls, and, once, a lady's bra… It is possible to diagnose a dog with an intestinal obstruction across a waiting room from a particularly 'tucked-up' stance and pained facial expression. These patients bounce back from surgery dramatically. A previously docile and compliant obstructed patient will return for a post-operative check-up and literally bounce into the consulting room.

- External: Grass awns are adept at finding their way into orifices such as a nostril, down an ear, and into the soft skin between two digits (toes), whence they start a one-way journey due to the direction of their whiskers.

In particular, I remember a grass awn that migrated from a hindpaw, causing abscesses along the way but not yielding itself up until it erupted through the skin in the groin!

GASTRIC DILATION/ VOLVULUS

This condition, commonly known as bloat or gastric torsion, is where the stomach swells visibly (dilatation) and then rotates (volvulus), so that the exit into the small intestine becomes blocked, preventing food from leaving. This results in stomach pain and a bloated abdomen. It is a severe, life-threatening condition that requires immediate veterinary attention (usually surgery).

There appears to be several risk factors causing the development of GDV. Feeding two smaller meals each day instead of one large one can help, as can preventing the dog from drinking a large volume of water at one time. Most importantly, you should never feed your Siberian immediately before or after strenuous exercise – wait at least two hours. Stress is also a significant factor, so make sure your Husky has the right care and lifestyle.

The signs of bloat vary, but the dog will generally seem unlike his

GASTRITIS

This is usually a simple stomach upset, most commonly in response to dietary indiscretion. Scavenging constitutes a change in the diet as much as an abrupt switch in the food being fed by the owner. There are also some specific infections causing more severe gastritis/enteritis, which will require treatment from a veterinary surgeon (see also Canine Parvovirus under 'Vaccination' on page 133).

Generally, a day without food, followed by a few days of small, frequent meals of a bland diet (such as cooked chicken or fish), or an appropriate prescription diet, should allow the stomach to settle. It is vital to ensure the patient is drinking and retaining sufficient water to cover losses resulting from the stomach upset in addition to the normal losses to be expected when healthy. Oral rehydration fluid may not be very appetising for the patient, in which case cooled boiled water should be offered. Fluids should initially be offered in small but frequent amounts to avoid over-drinking, which can result in further vomiting and thereby dehydration and electrolyte imbalances. It is also important to wean the patient back on to routine food gradually or else another bout of gastritis may occur.

usual self – miserable and restless, perhaps whining, pacing, or licking the air. He may have a hunched up appearance and attempt to vomit or defaecate repeatedly - usually unsuccessfully. He may also start breathing very shallowly, coughing and drooling. If you ever suspect bloat, you should get your dog to a vet immediately, as the condition progresses very rapidly (sometimes within minutes) and left untreated it is fatal.

HEATSTROKE

Heatstroke can kill. Care must be taken when exercising in hot weather so that the dog does not overheat. He must have access to fresh drinking water and shade. Like all breeds, a Siberian should never be left in a hot car.

Do not make the mistake of clipping or shaving your Siberian's thick coat during the summer months to help him keep cool. The undercoat keeps him cool during summer as well as warm in winter. Shaving your Husky can contribute to heat stroke rather than prevent it.

Signs of heatstroke include excessive panting, progressing to drooling, vomiting, diarrhoea, and ultimately death. If you suspect your Siberian is overheating, get him in the shade and give him plenty to drink. Give him a cool bath if you can, but if he doesn't improve rapidly, or you think he already has heatstroke (rather than simply being hot), contact a veterinary surgeon immediately.

JOINT PROBLEMS

It is not unusual for older Siberian Huskies to be stiff after exercise, particularly in cold weather. Your veterinary surgeon will be able to advise you on ways of helping your dog cope with stiffness, not least of which will be to ensure that he is not overweight. Arthritic joints do not need to be burdened with extra bodyweight!

LUMPS

Regularly handling and stroking your dog will enable the early detection of lumps and bumps. These may be due to infection (abscess), bruising, multiplication of particular cells from within the body, or even an external parasite (tick). If you are worried about any lump you find, have it checked by a veterinary surgeon.

OBESITY

Being overweight predisposes to many other problems, such as diabetes mellitus, heart disease and joint problems. It is easily prevented. Ignore pleading eyes and feed according to your dog's waistline. The body condition is what matters qualitatively, alongside monitoring that individual's bodyweight as a quantitative measure. The Siberian Husky should, in my opinion as a health professional, have at least a suggestion of a waist and it should be possible to feel the ribs beneath only a slight layer of fat.

Neutering does not mean that your Siberian will be overweight. Having an ovario-hysterectomy does slow down the body's rate of working, castration to a lesser extent, but it therefore means that your dog needs less food. I recommend cutting back on the amount of food fed a few weeks before neutering to accustom your Siberian Husky to less food. If she looks a little underweight on the morning of the operation, it will help the veterinary surgeon as well as giving her a little leeway weight-wise afterwards. It is always harder to lose weight after neutering than before, because of this slowing in the body's inherent metabolic rate.

TEETH PROBLEMS

Eating food starts with the canine teeth gripping and killing prey in the wild, incisor teeth biting off pieces of food and the molar teeth chewing it. To be able to eat is

If tartar and plaque are allowed to build up, tooth decay and gum infection will result.

vital for life, yet the actual health of the teeth is often overlooked: unhealthy teeth can predispose to disease, and not just by reducing the ability to eat. The presence of infection within the mouth can lead to bacteria entering the bloodstream and then filtering out at major organs, with the potential for serious consequences. That is not to forget that simply having dental pain can affect a dog's wellbeing, as anyone who has had toothache will confirm.

Veterinary dentistry has made huge leaps in recent years, so that it no longer consists of extraction as the treatment of necessity. Good dental health lies in the hands of the owner, starting from the moment your bring the dog home. Just as we have taken on responsibility for feeding, so we have acquired the task of dental and oral hygiene. In an ideal world, we should brush our dogs' teeth as regularly as our own. However, this may require loads of patience when dealing with a Siberian Husky puppy who finds having his teeth brushed twice a day to be a huge game.

There are alternative strategies, ranging from dental chewsticks to specially formulated foods, but the main thing is to be aware of your dog's mouth. At least train your puppy to permit full examination of his teeth. This will not only ensure you are checking in his mouth regularly but will also make your veterinary surgeon's job easier when your dog has to 'open wide!'

INHERITED DISORDERS

Fortunately, the Siberian Husky is a very healthy breed, with few inherited disorders. However, the presence of inherited disorders has significant implications for the affected dog and for any future offspring. There are control schemes in place for some conditions, such as hip dysplasia (see page 143) and various eye conditions (see below).

To date, a few inherited conditions have been identified in the Siberian Husky. **Hereditary cardiac hypertrophy** and **increased platelet aggregation** may be physiological adaptations arising from the development of the Siberian Husky as an endurance breed.

EYE TESTING

Siberian Huskies can suffer from some hereditary eye diseases and all Sibes should have their eyes tested by a KC-approved opthalmologist at 12 months. Dogs that are likely to be used for breeding should have their eyes tested annually.

In the UK, the British Veterinary Association, Kennel Club

and International Sheep Dog Society jointly run an eye screening scheme to check for inherited abnormalities.

In the US, a similar scheme is run by the Canine Eye Registration Foundation (CERF). This was set up by dog breeders concerned about heritable eye disease, and provides a database of dogs who have been examined by diplomates of the American College of Veterinary Ophthalmologists.

In alphabetical order, eye conditions of significance include:

Canine Uveodermatological Syndrome (Vogt-Koyanagi-Harada-like syndrome):

There is a breed predisposition to this autoimmune condition. It targets the pigment cells or melanocytes. As well as loss of pigment in the skin, there is uveitis or inflammation of the iris of the eye, which can lead to blindness. It affects young adult dogs.

Cataract: This is thought to be inherited in an autosomal recessive fashion. Cataract formation is at the back of the lens from six months of age, and can affect vision. Cataracts are one of the eye conditions that can be screened for.

Corneal Lipid Dystrophy: A recessive form of inheritance has

The Siberian Husky is still a sound breed with few inherited disorders, because the need to produce a healthy working dog led to careful selection and health testing of breeding stock.

been proposed in the Siberian Husky for this disorder of the cornea, the outermost layer of the eye. The type of corneal lipid dystrophy affecting the husky does not usually affect the vision or cause problems. White or off-white crystalline deposits of lipid, often cholesterol, are laid down within the cornea of one or both eyes. There is a wide range in age for when it manifests, from puppyhood onwards.

Entropion: This is an inrolling of the eyelids. It is usually the lower eyelids that are affected. There are degrees of entropion, ranging from

a slight inrolling to the more serious case, requiring surgical correction because of the pain and damage to the surface of the eye.

Generalised Progressive Retinal Atrophy (GPRA): The effects of the changes within the retina become apparent in the young adult It is inherited as an X-linked factor in the Siberian Husky, males being more often affected than females. Initially night vision is lost, which eventually can lead to total blindness.

Glaucoma: This is when the pressure of the fluid within the eyeball rises. It is a very painful condition, which can lead to blindness in the affected eye(s) if left untreated. It is controlled under the British Veterinary Association/Kennel Club/International Sheepdog Society Eye Scheme in the UK.

Pannus: The textbook name **chronic superficial keratitis** describes this condition, namely a long-term inflammation of the cornea. There is often a conjunctivitis or inflammation of the conjunctiva as well. The extent of the inflammation varies between affected individuals. Ultimately, blindness can result.

Treatment is mainly a management consideration, in an attempt to limit the effects and progression of the inflammation. Exposure to ultra-violet light waves may play a role so that minimising time spent in full sun is advised, keeping exercise to the early morning or evening.

Persistent Pupillary Membrane: During development within the womb, the eye is provided with blood by a membrane covering the pupil. This membrane usually breaks down before the puppy is born, although some strands may be present until four or five weeks of age. When strands remain beyond this age, they are called persistent pupillary membranes, and have a variable effect on vision depending on their location.

This condition is controlled in the Siberian Husky under Schedule B of the BVA/KC/ISDS Eye Scheme in the UK.

EPILEPSY
True epilepsy occurs in the Siberian Husky, manifesting between six months to three years of age. It is thought to be inherited.

ESSENTIAL HYPERTENSION
A hereditary form of essential hypertension (raised blood pressure) occurring from middle-age onwards has been found in a line of Siberian Huskies. The male may be predisposed.

HAEMOPHILIA A
Haemophilia is the most common disorder of blood coagulation. There are two forms of haemophilia, both of which are sex-linked recessive traits, carried on the X chromosome. This

HYPOTHYROIDISM

Siberian Huskies have a tendency to be more prone to an underactive thyroid gland than some other breeds, and although there is evidence that a lower level of thyroid hormones than usual is normal for sled dogs, Siberians can be vulnerable to a thyroid malfunction which owners need to be aware of.

The thyroid gland produces a hormone called thyroxine which affects many different parts of the body, and if a dog doesn't have enough thryoxine in his or blood the results can be very serious.

The main symptoms to look out for are:
• Lethargy and unusual tiredness
• Cold intolerance
• Thinning coat, especially on the tail and flanks
• Putting on weight or losing weight
• Lack of appetite or constant hunger
• A 'tragic' expression on the dog's face as if he or she is about to cry
• In bitches, abnormal or absent seasons
• In dogs, shrunken and soft testicles
• A nasty 'mousy' smell to the coat (although this is usually only in the later stages of the disease if it remains untreated).

In other breeds of dog hypothyrodism almost always causes the dog to become obese and his or her coat to become thin. Siberians do not always follow this pattern however, and they can actually be almost manic, lose weight and grow a heavier, coarser coat than usual. Because of this, if your dog seems to tire easily and is behaving oddly it is worth asking your vet to test for hypothyroidism just in case this is the cause.

If your dog does have low thyroxine levels further blood tests will be needed to determine exactly what is happening in his or her body. Once a full diagnosis has been made replacement hormone is given in the form of a small tablet each day and this is an effective treatment which is usually continued for the rest of the dog's life.

means that bitches can be carriers whilst a male carrying one of the genes will be affected. Fortunately, haemophilia is extremely rare.

In classic haemophilia or haemophilia A, there is a deficiency of blood-clotting factor VIII. There are many ways in which haemophilia A can manifest, ranging from a mild bleeding disorder to, at worst, sudden death. There may be early indications, such as prolonged bleeding when the baby teeth are lost or unexpected bruising under the skin. A problem may not become apparent until after surgery, such as routine neutering or an injury. Treatment will often require a blood transfusion.

HIP DYSPLASIA (HD)

This is any abnormality of one or both hip joints. In severe cases, the dog will find it extremely difficult and painful to walk and the kindest/only solution may be to end the dog's suffering. Mildly affected dogs may show no signs and lead a normal life, although arthritis of the joints may develop in later life.

Although known to be hereditary, environmental effects during the rapid growth phase of a young dog, such as over-exercise, excessive weight and poor nutrition, can contribute. Gentle exercise, reduction in obesity, anti-inflammatory drugs and home management are all part of the treatment regimes used to control the disease in mild to moderate cases, though for many dogs expensive surgery will be required. Sadly, for dogs affected more

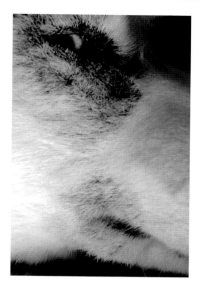

A zinc deficiency may result in itchiness and fur loss around the eye and/or mouth

severely, there is no treatment, which is why it is so important for breeders to screen their dogs for HD and why prospective owners should take care to source their dogs from reputable sources.

There are two main screening programmes for hip dysplasia. In the UK, the hips will be assessed by X-ray under the British Veterinary Association/Kennel Club scheme. An average (or mean) score is calculated for all breeds scored under the scheme and advice for breeders is to use only breeding stock with scores well below the breed mean score.

In the US, hip scoring is carried out by the Orthopedic Foundation for Animals. X-rays are submitted when a dog is two years old, and the dog will be graded.

For more detail about the scoring/grading systems, see page 50. Further information about both schemes can be obtained from the organisations involved.

LARYNGEAL PARALYSIS

There is an inherited form of laryngeal paralysis in the Siberian Husky, which manifests before six months of age. It is a very distressing condition for both dog and owner. Malfunction of the muscles responsible for opening the larynx as part of normal breathing results in a varying degree of airway obstruction. Respiration is noisy and laboured. There may be gagging whilst eating, coughing and an altered bark. Exercise, stress and hot weather are factors that can exacerbate the problem and an affected dog may collapse, requiring emergency treatment. It is possible to perform surgery on the larynx to ease the problem.

DEGENERATIVE MYELOPATHY (CDRM)

Chronic degenerative radiculo-myelopathy affects medium and large breeds including the Siberian Husky. It affects the hindlimbs, manifesting from middle-age as a slowly progressive weakness and loss of hindlimb co-ordination, leading on to muscle wastage and ultimately an inability to walk over the course of a year or so. The affected dog is still able to control urination and defaecation but becomes less able to move to the designated area and to adopt the appropriate posture to pass urine and faeces. Various treatments have been proposed, but it is generally a matter of helping the dog to cope.

SKIN CONDITIONS

There are a number of skin disorders occurring in the Siberian Husky that may have an hereditary basis.

Zinc-responsive dermatosis:
One of the most common problems Siberian owners come across is a tendency to scabby, itchy skin that if left untreated can spread and cause bleeding and eventually baldness. This condition isn't always recognised at first by vets because it is almost unique to Northern breeds and is more an adaptation to their original environment than a disease.

Some people call this condition zinc deficiency but, in fact, it is not a deficiency, rather an inability to digest zinc unless high levels of vitamin A are also present in the diet. This is probably because the natural diet of the early northern sled dogs was blubber, fish and liver, all high in both zinc and vitamin A. Over centuries the dogs adapted to this diet and nowadays, when fed a normal balanced food, some of them are unable to digest sufficient zinc to keep their skin healthy.

ZRD usually (but not always) appears as a scabby, bald area around the lips, eyes and/or nose. It can also start on the feet and around the genitals. The scabs are itchy and can often bleed if scratched or rubbed.

The usual treatment is a zinc supplement which is available from vets. Just using zinc from a human health food shop is not suitable because the amount of

A Siberian with snow nose will lose pigment in the winter months, but the colour may get darker again in the summer. This is normal for the breed.

zinc needs to be balanced with the correct amount of vitamin A. You can also help by adding fresh oily fish to your dog's diet or by choosing a fish-based kibble. For more serious cases a small piece of liver (about the size of a 50p piece) daily as a treat will help enormously and when lightly grilled most dogs love it.

ZRD can take a long time to improve, and you must keep up with any supplements your vet recommends plus regular oily fish and liver for several months to see a good response. Most Siberians do not have ZRD symptoms all the time, and especially in bitches they come and go with the seasons, so you are unlikely to have to give supplements continually. It is however, a good idea to keep the possibility that an itchy skin condition could be zinc related and ask your vet to eliminate ZRD from the list of possibilities when trying to find a cause.

Follicular dysplasia: This may affect several puppies in a litter from three to four months of age. The primary hairs on the body fall out and are not replaced, and there is reddening of the undercoat. Fur tends not to grow back after being clipped. The fur on the head and lower parts of the legs is spared.

Snow nose: This is a particular form of nasal depigmentation, that occurs in the Siberian Husky. The nose becomes a lighter colour during winter with a return to the darker colour possible in the summer.

Canine eosinophilic granuloma: This is a rare condition of unknown cause. Red or yellow skin nodules causing variable itchiness occur on the inner aspect of the thighs or inside the mouth, and respond to treatment with corticosteroids. There is a male predisposition.

Discoid Lupus Erythematosus: This immune-mediated skin disease is centred on the nose and face. The Siberian Husky is over-represented in case studies of this condition.

There is depigmentation of the nose, which loses its usual characteristic appearance, becoming grey, smooth and often ulcerated. The lips, ears and external genitalia may also become affected, and there may be thickening of the footpads. It is exacerbated by exposure to sunlight, so can be confused with solar dermatitis. Treatment includes the use of appropriate sunscreens and avoiding sunlight when possible. Corticosteroids can be effective when applied as a cream, limited by the likelihood of being licked away, or may need to be taken by mouth.

COMPLEMENTARY THERAPIES

Just as for human health, I do believe that there is a place for alternative therapies alongside and complementing orthodox treatment under the supervision of a veterinary surgeon. Because animals do not have a choice, there are measures in place to safeguard their wellbeing and welfare. All manipulative treatment (e.g. physiotherapy) must be under the direction of a veterinary surgeon. All other complementary therapies, such as acupuncture, homoeopathy and aromatherapy, can only be carried out by veterinary surgeons who have been trained in that particular field.

SUMMARY

As the owner of a Siberian Husky, you are responsible for his care and health. Not only must you make decisions on his behalf, you are also responsible for establishing a lifestyle for him that will ensure he leads a long and happy life. Diet plays an important a part in this, as does exercise.

For the domestic dog, it is only in recent years that the need has been recognised for changing the diet to suit the dog as he grows, matures and then enters his

With good care and management, your Siberian should live a long, happy and healthy life.

twilight years. So-called life-stage diets try to match the nutritional needs of the dog as he progresses through life.

An adult dog food will suit the Siberian Husky living a standard family life. There are also foods for those Siberian Huskies tactfully termed as obese-prone, such as those who have been neutered or are less active than others, or simply like their food. Do remember, though, that ultimately you are in control of your Siberian Husky's diet, unless he is able to profit from scavenging!

On the other hand, prescription diets are of necessity fed under the supervision of a veterinary

surgeon because each is formulated to meet the very specific needs of particular health conditions. Should a prescription diet be fed to a healthy dog, or to a dog with a different illness, there could be adverse effects.

It is important to remember that your Siberian Husky has no choice. As his owner, you are responsible for any decision made, so it must be as informed a decision as possible. Always speak to your vet if you have any worries about your Siberian Husky. He is not just a dog; from the moment you brought him home, he became a member of the family.

THE CONTRIBUTORS

THE EDITORS: NICKY HUTCHISON

Nicky has owned and worked her Siberian Huskies for a number of years and spent some time in Alaska helping to train dogs for the Iditarod sled dog race.

Nicky is a dog trainer and Regional Manager for the national training organisation Puppy School and is a member of the Association of Pet Dog Trainers. She is a major advocate for kind, gentle training to get the best out of huskies.

Nicky introduced the sport of Canicross to the UK and likes nothing better than running (and chasing the odd squirrel) on forest trails with her lovely huskies.

THE EDITORS: HELEN WOOD

Helen Wood and her partner Paul Norris, whose photographs illustrate much of this book, went to their first husky rally in Kielder in 1989, thinking that they might get some decent pictures because of the snow. They did, and four years later they bought their first Siberian, starting on the slippery slope to van-owning and poverty! They currently have six Sibes that have been both worked and shown, making up a champion, Ch Penkhala's Seska (Page 6) in 2009, who also made the top 10 of the Dual Championship in the following season.

HELEN AND JOHN GUTTERIDGE

In the 1960s and 70s Helen had beagles and a basenji, along with a small collection of reptiles and amphibians. In the mid 1970s she began her education in Siberian Huskies, acquiring her first in 1982. Since then she has shown, raced, bred and judged them in the UK, giving her first set of Challenge Certificates in 1992.

In the working arena, Siberians of her breeding have won many races, including Championship series. In showing she has several in the KC stud book, most notably Qiqern Kakwik.

She lectures on the Breed Standard,

structure and gait on behalf of the Siberian Husky Club of Great Britain.

She practises as a registered Podiatrist in the Northwest of England, living with her husband John and their current two dogs, Beamer and Gibbs.
See Chapter Seven: The Perfect Siberian Husky

CUSHLA LAMEN

Cushla grew up with a variety of pets, although her primary love has always been dogs. Her first dog of choice with her husband was a Siberian Husky. They have since had the pleasure of sharing their lives with several huskies all of which have had very different characters and personalities.

Cushla is a Gwen Bailey Puppy School tutor, providing reward based training and socialisation during the vital, early developmental period for all breeds of puppies. Cushla also offers one to one dog training and is one of the founding members of Canicross Trailrunners, the only Kennel Club accredited 'cross country running with dogs' group. Cushla regularly competes at Canicross with her own dogs, both in the United Kingdom and abroad and is proud of her huskies' achievements across a variety of distances, including completing some ultra distances, which her dogs excel at.

Cushla is passionate about the well-being of dogs and is a qualified Galen Myotherapist. She uses these canine massage skills to help keep her own dogs in the best possible condition and to treat a wide variety of veterinary referrals. Cushla is member of CAAM, The Canine Association of Accredited Myotherapsts.

CHRIS McRAE (ZOOX)

Chris McRae owned her first dog when she was 16, starting out in obedience. Chris and husband Ian started to show and work their Samoyeds in 1976, and 2 years later Aneka, their first Siberian, came into their lives. The Zoox/Zateizzi kennel is responsible for 24 champions, 4 Samoyeds and 20 Siberians, of which 22 were home bred. Chris and Zoox

Gadzheek won the first CC awarded to Siberian Huskies in Britain at Crufts 1986. He became a Champion and sired 5 Champions. She judged the breed at Crufts in 1990, and judges overseas. One of Chris's own Siberians gained her KC Good Citizen Gold when she was just 7 months old.

Teams led by or fully made up of Zoox/Zateizzi dogs have won 59 races and finished in the top three 154 times in the last eight years. In 1985 the SHCGB approved the Complete Siberian Husky award based on a dogs wins in the ring and on the trail, this was won by Zoox Gadzheek, a similar award still runs, now called The Dual Champion and in 20011 it was again won by a Zoox Champion.

JULIA BARNES

Julia has owned and trained a number of different dog breeds, and has also worked as a puppy socialiser for Dogs for the Disabled. A former journalist, she has written many books, including several on dog training and behaviour. Julia is indebted to Nicky Hutchison for her specialist knowledge about Siberian Huskies.
See Chapter Six: Training and Socialisation.

ALISON LOGAN MA VetMB MRCVS

Alison qualified as a veterinary surgeon from Cambridge University in 1989, having been brought up surrounded by all manner of animals and birds in the north Essex countryside. She has been in practice in her home town ever since, living with her husband, two children and Labrador Retriever Pippin.

She contributes on a regular basis to *Veterinary Times, Veterinary Nurse Times, Dogs Today, Cat World* and *Pet Patter*, the PetPlan newsletter. In 1995, Alison won the Univet Literary Award with an article on Cushing's Disease, and she won it again (as the Vetoquinol Literary Award) in 2002, writing about common conditions in the Shar-Pei.
See Chapter Eight: Happy and Healthy.

USEFUL ADDRESSES

KENNEL & BREED CLUBS

UK
The Kennel Club
1 Clarges Street, London, W1J 8AB
Tel: 0870 606 6750
Fax: 0207 518 1058
Web: www.the-kennel-club.org.uk

To obtain up-to-date contact information for the following breed clubs, contact the Kennel Club:
- Scottish Siberian Husky Club
- Siberian Husky Club of Great Britain
  (www.siberianhuskyclub.com)

USA
American Kennel Club (AKC)
5580 Centerview Drive,
Raleigh, NC 27606, USA.
Tel: 919 233 9767
Email: info@akc.org
Web: www.akc.org

United Kennel Club (UKC)
100 E Kilgore Rd, Kalamazoo,
MI 49002-5584, USA.
Tel: 269 343 9020
Web:www.ukcdogs.com/

Siberian Husky Club of America, Inc.
Web: http://www.shca.org/

For contact details of regional clubs, please contact the Siberian Husky Club of America.

AUSTRALIA
Australian National Kennel Council (ANKC)
The Australian National Kennel Council is the administrative body for pure breed canine affairs in Australia. It does not, however, deal directly with dog exhibitors, breeders or judges. For information pertaining to breeders, clubs or shows, please contact the relevant State or Territory Controlling Body.

Dogs Australian Capital Territory
PO Box 815, Dickson ACT 2602
Tel: (02) 6241 4404
Fax: (02) 6241 1129
Email: administrator@dogsact.org.au
Web: www.dogsact.org.au

Dogs New South Wales
PO Box 632, St Marys, NSW 1790
Tel: (02) 9834 3022 or 1300 728 022 (NSW Only)
Email: info@dogsnsw.org.au
Web: www.dogsnsw.org.au

Dogs Northern Territory
PO Box 37521, Winnellie NT 0821
Tel: (08) 8984 3570
Fax: (08) 8984 3409

Email: admin@dogsnt.com.au
Web: www.dogsnt.com.au

Dogs Queensland
PO Box 495, Fortitude Valley Qld 4006
Tel: (07) 3252 2661
Fax: (07) 3252 3864
Email: info@dogsqueensland.org.au
Web: www.dogsqueensland.org.au

Dogs South Australia
PO Box 844, Prospect East SA 5082
Tel: (08) 8349 4797
Fax: (08) 8262 5751
Email: info@dogssa.com.au
Web: www.dogssa.com.au

Tasmanian Canine Association Inc
The Rothman Building
PO Box 116, Glenorchy Tas 7010
Tel: (03) 6272 9443
Fax: (03) 6273 0844
Email: tca@iprimus.com.au
Web: www.tasdogs.com

Dogs Victoria
Locked Bag K9
Cranbourne VIC 3977
Tel: (03)9788 2500
Fax: (03) 9788 2599
Email: office@dogsvictoria.org.au
Web: www.dogsvictoria.org.au

Dogs Western Australia
PO Box 1404, Canning Vale WA 6970
Tel: (08) 9455 1188
Fax: (08) 9455 1190
Email: k9@dogswest.com
Web: www.dogswest.com

INTERNATIONAL
Fédération Cynologique Internationalé (FCI)/World Canine Organisation
Place Albert 1er, 13, B-6530 Thuin,
Belgium.
Tel: +32 71 59.12.38
Fax: +32 71 59.22.29
Web: www.fci.be/

RESCUE ORGANISATIONS
UK
www.shcgbwelfare.org.uk
http://www.dogstrust.org.uk/

USA
www.siberianrescue.com

AUSTRALIA
Please contact the relevant State or Territory controlling body to find the rescue section of your local club.

TRAINING AND BEHAVIOUR

UK
Association of Pet Dog Trainers
PO Box 17, Kempsford, GL7 4WZ
Telephone: 01285 810811
Email: APDToffice@aol.com
Web: http://www.apdt.co.uk

Association of Pet Behaviour Counsellors
PO BOX 46, Worcester, WR8 9YS
Telephone: 01386 751151
Fax: 01386 750743
Email: info@apbc.org.uk
Web: http://www.apbc.org.uk/

USA
Association of Pet Dog Trainers
101 North Main Street, Suite 610
Greenville, SC 29601, USA.
Tel: 1 800 738 3647
Email: information@apdt.com
Web: www.apdt.com/

American College of Veterinary Behaviorists
College of Veterinary Medicine, 4474 Tamu, Texas A&M University
College Station, Texas 77843-4474
Web: http://dacvb.org/

American Veterinary Society of Animal Behavior
Web: www.avsabonline.org/

AUSTRALIA
APDT Australia Inc
PO Box 3122, Bankstown Square, NSW 2200,
Email: secretary@apdt.com.au
Web: www.apdt.com.au

Canine Behaviour
For details of regional behaviourists, contact the relevant State or Territory Controlling Body.

ACTIVITIES &V INFORMATION

UK
All activites and general information
www.sibespace.co.uk

Agility
http://www.agilityclub.co.uk/

Canicross
www.canicrosstrailrunners.org.uk
www.cani-cross.co.uk

Flyball
Web: http://www.flyball.org.uk/

Sled Dog Activities & Equipment
www.huskyracing.org.uk

www.sdas.org.uk
www.absasleddogracing.org.uk
www.amwa.org.uk
www.leaddog-training.com
www.sassdogequipment.co.uk
www.facebook.com/trailbabysleddog.k9gear
www.countryhounds.co.uk
www.snowpawstore.com
www.snopeak.co.uk

USA
Agility
www.nadac.com/

Flyball
www.flyball.org/

Sled Dog Activities & Equipment
www.urbanmushing.com
http://americanmusher.webs.com/
www.sleddogcentral.com/

Further information, particularly about organisations in your area, can be obtained by contacting the Siberian Husky Club of America.

AUSTRALIA
Agility
www.adaa.com.au/
www.nadacaustralia.com/

Flyball
www.flyball.org.au/

Sled Dog Activities & Equipment
Information can be obtained by contacting the relevant State or Territory controlling body or the Australian Sled Dog Sports Association:
http://assa.heavenforum.org/

INTERNATIONAL
World Canine Freestyle Organisation
Web: www.worldcaninefreestyle.org

International Federation of Sled Dog Sports
http://www.sleddogsport.net/

International Sled Dog Racing Association
http://www.isdra.org/default.asp

HEALTH

UK
Alternative Veterinary Medicine Centre
Chinham House, Stanford in the Vale, Oxfordshire, SN7 8NQ
Tel: 01367 710324
Fax: 01367 718243
Web: www.alternativevet.org/

British Small Animal Veterinary Association
Woodrow House, 1 Telford Way, Waterwells Business Park, Quedgeley, Gloucestershire, GL2 2AB

Tel: 01452 726700
Email: customerservices@bsava.com
Web: http://www.bsava.com/

Royal College of Veterinary Surgeons
Belgravia House, 62-64 Horseferry Road, London, SW1P 2AF
Tel: 0207 222 2001
Email: admin@rcvs.org.uk
Web: www.rcvs.org.uk

USA
American Holistic Veterinary Medical Association
2218 Old Emmorton Road
Bel Air, MD 21015
Tel: 410 569 0795
Email: office@ahvma.org
Web: www.ahvma.org/

American Veterinary Medical Association
1931 North Meacham Road, Suite 100, Schaumburg, IL 60173-4360, USA.
Tel: 800 248 2862
Web: www.avma.org

American College of Veterinary Surgeons
19785 Crystal Rock Dr, Suite 305
Germantown, MD 20874, USA.
Tel: 301 916 0200
Toll Free: 877 217 2287
Email: acvs@acvs.org
Web: www.acvs.org/

AUSTRALIA
Australian Holistic Vets
Web: www.ahv.com.au/

Australian Small Animal Veterinary Association
40/6 Herbert Street, St Leonards, NSW 2065, Australia.
Tel: 02 9431 5090
Email: asava@ava.com.au
Web: www.asava.com.au

Australian Veterinary Association
Unit 40, 6 Herbert Street, St Leonards, NSW 2065, Australia.
Tel: 02 9431 5000
Fax: 02 9437 9068
Web: www.ava.com.au

Australian College Veterinary Scientists
Building 3, Garden City Office Park, 2404 Logan Road, Eight Mile Plains, Queensland 4113, Australia.
Tel: 07 3423 2016
Email: admin@acvs.org.au
Web: http://acvsc.org.au

ASSISTANCE DOGS

UK
Canine Partners
Mill Lane, Heyshott, Midhurst, GU29 0ED

Tel: 08456 580480
Web: www.caninepartners.co.uk

Dogs for the Disabled
The Frances Hay Centre, Blacklocks Hill, Banbury, Oxon, OX17 2BS
Tel: 01295 252600
Web: www.dogsforthedisabled.org

Guide Dogs for the Blind Association
Burghfield Common, Reading, RG7 3YG
Tel: 01189 835555
Web: www.guidedogs.org.uk/

Hearing Dogs for Deaf People
The Grange, Wycombe Road, Saunderton, Princes Risborough, Bucks, HP27 9NS
Tel: 01844 348100
Web: www.hearingdogs.org.uk

Pets as Therapy
14a High Street, Wendover, Aylesbury, Bucks. HP22 6EA.
Tel: 01845 345445
Web: http://www.petsastherapy.org/

Support Dogs
21 Jessops Riverside, Brightside Lane, Sheffield, S9 2RX
Tel: 01142 617800
Email: supportdogs@btconnect.com
Web: www.support-dogs.org.uk

USA
Therapy Dogs International
88 Bartley Road, Flanders, NJ 07836,.
Tel: 973 252 9800
Web: www.tdi-dog.o

Therapy Dogs Inc.
P.O. Box 20227, Cheyenne, WY 82003.
Tel: 307 432 0272.
Web: www.therapydogs.com

Delta Society - Pet Partners
875 124th Ave NE, Suite 101, Bellevue, WA 98005 USA.
Email: info@DeltaSociety.org
Web: www.deltasociety.org

Comfort Caring Canines
8135 Lare Street, Philadelphia, PA 19128.
Email: ccc@comfortcaringcanines.org
Web: www.comfortcaringcanines.org/

AUSTRALIA
AWARE Dogs Australia, Inc
PO Box 883, Kuranda, Queensland, 488..
Tel: 07 4093 8152
Web: www.awaredogs.org.au/

Delta Society — Therapy Dogs
Web: www.deltasociety.com.au